Preaching Biblical Sermons

Three Contemporary Strategies

RAYMOND O. BYSTROM

WINNIPEG, MB  HILLSBORO, KS

Published simultaneously by Kindred Books, an imprint of Kindred Productions, Winnipeg, Manitoba R3M 3Z6 and Kindred Productions, Hillsboro, Kansas 67063.

Cover and Book Design: Fred Koop, Saskatoon, SK
Printed by Blitzprint, Calgary, AB

Library and Archives Canada Cataloguing in Publication

Bystrom, Raymond O.
    Preaching biblical sermons : three contemporary strategies / Raymond O. Bystrom.

Includes bibliographical references.
ISBN 1-894791-11-8

        1. Preaching. I. Title.
BV4211.3.B97 2006   251   C2006-902184-8

Table of Contents

Preface

This book has its origins in my career as a pastor, preacher, and teacher. My initial interest in preaching roots back to my Bible College days in the '60s. Since that time, my career has straddled the church and academy. Indeed, at times, I didn't know whether my place was in the church or in a college or seminary. But I have always had an interest in preaching, either as a pastor or professor.

After a decade of teaching biblical studies at Vancouver Bible College, Regent College and Trinity Western University (1971-81), I became a pastor and served two Mennonite Brethren congregations in British Columbia for the better part of a decade. As a pastor, I was faced with the challenge of getting the message of the Bible heard by the varieties of listeners sitting before me each Sunday.

Gordon Fee once made a telltale remark about preaching that encouraged me to revise my preaching strategy. Speaking of sermon construction, he wrote:

> "Remember that a well-told story (that is relevant to the text!) will be remembered far longer than your finest prose. Be sure you do not go too long into the sermon without the break that a good, helpful illustration affords, both to enlighten your point and to relieve the minds of those who are trying to follow your logic. For help in this area, consult the better books on homiletics" (1983: 136).

One day, after reading Fee's statement, I took the time

to examine a few of my sermons. His remarks hit home. I was employing a strategy that was little more than three burdensome logical points with helpful illustrations designed to relieve the minds of those who were trying to follow my logic. I took Fee's advice and started consulting some of the better books on homiletics in an effort to find a fresh approach to preaching.

On the basis of book reviews found in preaching journals and advice from fellow pastors and former professors, I consulted works that introduced me to some of the alternatives to the discursive homiletic strategy that had dominated my preaching. Initially, I read Fred B. Craddock's book *Preaching*, which won the 1986 "Book of the Year" award from the publishers of a popular preaching journal that came to my mailbox every quarter. At the time, Craddock was Professor of New Testament and Preaching at Candler School of Theology at Emory University in Atlanta. Craddock has written other books on preaching, including *As One Without Authority* (1971) and *Overhearing the Gospel* (1978). As I read and studied his writings, I learned that he advocates an inductive approach to the preaching of biblical texts and questions the typical deductive style with which I was most familiar. Soon I was trying to implement his approach to preaching the Bible and often I received positive feedback from my listeners who noted the change in style.

In another preaching journal, I read that Eugene Lowry's method of preaching, "demands the attention and study of every serious proclaimer of the Word" (Blair 1982: 23). So I began to read and study his writings. He was Professor of Preaching at St. Paul School of Theology in Kansas City at the time. In particular, I studied the following books on preaching by Lowry: *The Homiletical Plot* (1980), *Doing Time in the Pulpit* (1985), *How to Preach a Parable* (1989), and *The Sermon: Dancing the Edge of Mystery* (1997). Again, I attempted to implement what I had been reading and studying, struggling to master Lowry's narrative approach to preaching the biblical text. To be sure, I failed many times, but once in awhile things came together and God's people heard the Bible's message in a fresh way.

My adventure of consulting the "better books" on preaching eventually led me to the writings of David Buttrick whose book, *Homiletic,* was hailed by *Christianity Today* as "one of the most important books on preaching to appear this century" (McCullough 1991: 8). Buttrick was Professor of Homiletics and Worship at Vanderbilt Divinity School in Nashville at the time. I also studied a few of his other books, including *Preaching Jesus Christ* (1988), *The Mystery and the Passion* (1992), and *Captive Voice* (1994). He believes biblical texts have movement and meaning occurs in movement as it travels from one understanding to another. He encourages preachers to favor mobile systems for sermon construction as opposed to fixed categorical development. Again, I began the arduous task of trying to implement his strategy, and occasionally I succeeded.

Eventually I completed a doctoral degree at Fuller Theological Seminary where I concentrated on the discipline of homiletics. Indeed, this book is a revision of my doctoral dissertation. I confess that I have enjoyed my homiletical journey, especially since I have had such great "friends" and "mentors" in persons like Fred Craddock, Eugene Lowry, and David Buttrick. And I am also grateful to the Mennonite Brethren congregations I mentioned earlier whose grace and patience gave me the freedom to experiment with new sermonic forms.

For the past 15 years (1991-2006) I have been serving at the Mennonite Brethren Biblical Seminary where I have had the delightful task of introducing my students to the preaching theories of homileticians like Craddock, Lowry, and Buttrick. In fact, I want to dedicate this book to the students of my preaching classes at MBBS, praying that this resource will help them in their preaching ministries.

Introduction

Preaching has been in the midst of a remarkable renewal in recent decades. It has experienced what some are calling a "Copernican Revolution" (Eslinger 1987: 65). Hundreds of new books on preaching have appeared in recent years. Seminaries are adding courses and faculty in homiletics. Journals, magazines and other helpful resources for preachers abound. And, most importantly, local congregations still insist on competent biblical preaching.

A few years ago, sermon content was everything. The current trend is toward sermonic form. Today sermon shape and structure occupy the honored seat in the creation of the sermon. Homileticians have been busy creating new sermon approaches. A few of the more prominent options include Fred Craddock's inductive method, Eugene Lowry's narrative sermonic plot, and David Buttrick's phenomenological approach.

Often preachers cling to a single sermonic form. An old orthodoxy of discursive preaching is especially prominent in our pulpits in North America. This model is built upon argument and organized by points and propositions. The sermon is frequently little more than three burdensome logical points with helpful illustrations designed to relieve the minds of those who are trying to follow the preacher's logic. Ironically, many preachers insist on using a single sermon form, an old rationalistic one at that, even though the current revolution in preaching offers them a plethora of new sermon forms that would help them get their message heard.

What makes this situation especially puzzling is that in everyday life people demand variety. Our church people work with compact disc players that shuffle ten or more discs and remote controls that enable them to surf hundreds of channels. They spend their money in stores the size of small countries because they demand variety in every area of life. I have friends who have four or five books on the go at the same time. When my wife goes to the grocery store she buys a variety of meats for the week because she wants variety at mealtime. God's people also deserve to have the bread of life dished out in diverse ways. It's time for preachers to recognize that there is no single sermonic form, but rather, a wide variety of living options available to them.

The premise of this book is simple. Today's church members are growing restless with a single approach to preaching. To get the truth heard by the varieties of listeners sitting before them each Sunday, preachers need to move beyond "three points and a poem." This book is a call for preachers to embrace a variety of sermonic forms.

At the outset, I will provide a sample sermon that exemplifies the discursive method that has dominated the homiletical horizon since the second century of the Christian era. Then I will briefly explain the reasons for the current shift to new sermonic forms.

Example of a Discursive Sermon

Here is an example of a discursive or deductive sermon I most often preached prior to my study of the three homileticians whose methods are described in the following pages. This sermon, which is based on the texts of Hosea 4:1-3, 6:6 and Matthew 9:9-13, was preached at the Cedar Park MB Church in Delta, British Columbia in 1990. I recognize that there is a legitimate place in the pulpit for sermons using the discursive method illustrated by this sermon. But I will argue in subsequent pages that preachers need to move beyond this single sermonic form.

Sermon
"What Really Matters?"

I want to speak this morning on the subject of loyalty and the need for loyalty in our lives before God. Sociologist Robert Bellah recently directed a research project on American values. To discover what Americans value, he interviewed well-educated middle-class Americans, many of them managers and therapists. He found the dominant value to be freedom, autonomy, and self-fulfillment. One young woman therapist from Atlanta sums up what he heard from many people: "In the end you're really alone," she said, "and you really have to answer to yourself. You're responsible for yourself and no one else" (1985:15).

Bellah is unhappy with this attitude because it undermines, at least potentially, every human commitment. If any person or group or institution doesn't meet my needs, if I don't feel good about them, if I don't feel comfortable with them, phrases he heard all the time, then there is no good reason I shouldn't leave. Thus, if marriage, friendship, job, community, and church don't meet my needs, I can always find others who will.

Well, that's something of the situation we are in today with the breakdown of so many of our social bonds. There is an absence of loyalty in all our relationships today, an absence of commitment and faithfulness to one another.

In today's Scripture lesson, the prophet Hosea laments the breakdown of social bonds in ancient Israel. "Hear the word of the Lord, you Israelites, because the Lord has a charge to bring against you who live in the land" (Hosea 4:1). With these words, God's people are ushered into an imaginary courtroom where they are charged before their judge on three accounts. First, "there is no faithfulness." Faithfulness refers to common honesty and reliability, the basic and foundational ingredient of all healthy human relationships. Second, "there is no love." This is an important word for Hosea. It speaks of the love and loyalty expected of partners in covenant relationships, especially loyalty to spouse, family, and friends, but preeminently, the loyalty we owe to the Lord as his people. Third, "there's no acknowledgement of God." This does not refer to a lack of head knowledge. The Hebrew people had lots of information about God. What they lacked, however, was obedience to God. They were living as if God did not exist. Here, then, is the root problem: there is neither loyalty to one another, nor loyalty to God.

The prophet then states that this absence of loyalty has a twofold result. First, "there is only cursing, lying and murder, stealing and adultery; they break all bounds, and bloodshed follows bloodshed." These are the evils the Ten Commandments urges God's people to avoid. So what we have here is a description of the complete breakdown of social boundaries; it's a picture of what happens when there is no faithfulness and commitment to one another as people. Second, "because of this," says the prophet, "the land mourns and all who live in it waste away; the beasts of the field and the birds of the air and the fish of the sea are dying." Here the prophet does an interesting thing. He links the environmental crisis with the breakdown in social relationships. Indeed, he speaks about the environment in a way that is very close to home. When there is no loyalty between people, there is no loyalty by the people to the land.

No wonder God says to his people, especially her leaders, "I desire loyalty not sacrifice, and acknowledgement of God rather than burnt offerings" (Hosea 6:6, NEB). Now we don't sacrifice animals or burnt offerings. What we do today, in most of our efforts at religious revival, is stimulate feelings. Although feeling good about God is not a bad thing, according to the prophet Hosea, the real measure of a true relationship with God is committed love and loyalty in all our relationships before Him.

So two questions for us to consider this morning: First, why is there so much disloyalty in our day? And second, why is loyalty so important for us as God's people? I would like to begin by considering the second question first—why is there so much disloyalty today?

I think one reason for the lack of loyalty in the land can be attributed to a number of conditions of our culture that tend to discourage healthy interpersonal relationships. For example, *work* has become increasingly specialized. Consequently, it is often necessary for us to travel great distances to get to our places of employment. We spend a great deal of time sitting in our automobiles. We have become a commuter society. Result: We have less time and energy for human relationships. We have less time for friends and family. While pastoring a church in Vancouver, I lived in the suburbs and drove to the church office five or six days a week. Each day I spent approximately two hours commuting to and from work. Result: I had less time and energy for spouse, children, and friends.

Then there's the *media*. Television talk shows and popular magazines give us the intimate details of the private lives of well-known people. We can spend a great deal of time learning about the intimate details of famous people and it becomes a kind of substitute for the hard work of developing two-way relationships. Result: We don't have to bother with two-way relationships that might cost us something in effort and time; we can get a vicarious sharing of other people's lives without effort.

Mobility is another characteristic of our culture that has the potential to undermine healthy interpersonal relationships. Automobiles, subways, and sky trains have made it easy for us to go to distant stores to do our shopping. In our home, if we happen to have a spare evening, we may choose to visit the biggest and newest shopping mall even if it is on the other side of the city. Result: There is little likelihood that we will meet someone that we know such as a neighbor or friend with whom we might talk and share our lives. Mobility does not necessarily enhance our opportunities for building relationships.

I must mention *consumerism* too. Advertising has taught us to look for happiness in things that can be bought. Externals are emphasized in our society. The old bumper sticker says it well: "Born to Shop." Result: Shopping and buying things often substitutes for the cultivation of friendships. Consumerism has also influenced our corporate life as God's people. Each congregation today is out on its own carving out its own market, winning its own clientele, and making its own appeal. Congregants have become customers. Result: If a church doesn't satisfy its customers, they go shopping elsewhere and relationships within the church are abandoned for the sake of a better deal down the street.

Then there is the *service* industry. There are so many service enterprises today that provide professional care, child care, food preparations, and home entertainment, to mention but a few. Result: We depend less and less on friends, relatives, and spouses to provide these services. We have come to depend on service industries rather than people.

I will mention one more. It's *change*. Change makes us fearful of becoming dependent on people and places. My wife and I have been married 25 years. Schooling, employment, and other factors prompted us to move homes 18 times during our married life. Result: Today we are less inclined to make emotional investments in either people or places. You see, we have experienced the pain of saying "good-bye" too many times. In this sense, change can discourage the cultivation of new friendships and loyalties.

Well, these are some of the reasons families and friends seem less necessary today. These are some of the things that can erode our loyalties and undermine our relationships.

But why be a loyal people? Why is loyalty so

important for us as God's people? First, loyalty is important because we are persons, not things. As persons we make claims upon one another. For example, at this moment I am claiming your attention. But you are also claiming my attention for you want me to stop speaking shortly so you can continue with the other activities of this day. As persons we make mutual and reciprocal claims upon one another.

When you leave church this morning you will not turn to your pew and thank it for holding you up because you are dealing with an object. But you might thank the person sitting next to you for joining you in worship today. So we do make claims upon one another because you and I are persons and we live with claims. That's why, in our Lord's Prayer, we are instructed to express our need for daily bread and food and our need to ask each other for forgiveness: "Forgive us the wrong we have done, as we have forgiven those who have wronged us" (Matthew 6:12).

Above all our God claims us because he is our Redeemer. He has bought us with a price—the price of his dear Son's life. And God's love brings its obligations—the obligation to respond by loving both God and our neighbors. So we cannot escape being claimed by one another and by our God.

Social analyst Daniel Yankelovich says that the "me-first" outlook on life is a candidate for the junk heap "because it is destructive both to the individual and to society. When one ceases to care about the world, the future, friends, and family, an essential part of the self vanishes" (1981: 236). So loyalty is important because it is intrinsic to our character as persons. As persons we cannot avoid making claims of loyalty upon one another.

There is at least one other reason why loyalty is so important for us. Loyalty is important because it is a mark of godliness. If we want to be a godly people, we must be a loyal people because God is loyal. Indeed, we could read the entire Bible in terms of God's covenant to be loyal to his people and his desire that his people be loyal to him and one another. For example, in the book of Ruth, we read about loyalty within the family. Ruth, having married is now widowed. She is legally dissolved of any further responsibility to her mother-in-law, Naomi. Yet she tells Naomi: "Where you go, I will go, and where you stay, I will stay. Your people will be my people, and your God my God" (Ruth 1:16). Later, Ruth marries Boaz. What happens at the end of this story of loyalty? Through Ruth's marriage to Boaz a son is born called Obed and Obed is father to Jesse who is father to David. From the seed of David comes David's greatest son—Jesus Christ. John tell us, in the prologue to his Gospel, that Jesus came into the world full of "loyalty and truth" (John 1:17, NEB). Think of how innocent Ruth was in her act of loyalty to Naomi. Yet, her loyalty gave birth to the Savior of the world!

Perhaps the most famous biblical story of loyalty between friends is the Old Testament story of David and Jonathan. How they loved one another. Young people, one of the most important things you can do at your stage of life is to find one or two friends and exercise this quality of loyalty with them. Next month, my wife and I will receive a visit from two very close friends whom we met while in college over 25 years ago—John and Sharon. Over the years, we have shared good times and tough times with them. They are people with whom we have some history. Through our friendship with John and Sharon we have learned a good deal about the sacramental character of friendship. Through our friendship with them we have experienced God's love with all of its power to heal and sustain. There's quite a lot in the New Testament about friendship, including the memorable suggestion by John's Gospel that Jesus sacrificed His life for the sake of his friends (John 15:15).

Speaking of Jesus, there is a wonderful story of loyalty in the marketplace that concerns him. In Matthew's Gospel, and on two occasions, Jesus reminds His friends "God desires loyalty not sacrifice" (9:13; 12:7, NEB). The first time he makes this statement he is eating a meal in the home of Matthew the tax collector. Now tax collectors were not generally known to be a loyal people. So the Pharisees complain that Jesus is eating and drinking with "sinners." Of course, in that ancient Palestinian culture, sharing a meal with someone carried great symbolic significance. By eating with these sinners, Jesus was signifying that he would be loyal to them and protect, even to the point of laying down his life for them.

Can you imagine how our corporate life as God's people would be transformed if the next time we shared a meal with someone we silently promised to be loyal to them—not to gossip about them, not to malign them, but instead to pray and stand by them come what may? If we could become a more loyal people, faithful in all of our relationships, the world would see more of Christ's likeness in us.

Well, Jesus was eating with those who were disloyal and his loyalty shines through in the midst of their disloyalty. Friends, the really "good news" in this story is that Jesus comes to people like you and me, shares his bread and cup with us, takes us by the hand, and then says, "Come, follow me. Come, follow me."

New Forms for the Sermon

There are at least three reasons for the emergence of new sermon forms in recent years: first, the pathology of the discursive method; second, the dynamics of the human listening process; and third, the fusion of biblical form and content. These three reasons together substantially explain the new interest in sermonic form.

1. The Pathology of the Discursive Method. Although a narrative sermonic structure was most characteristic of first century Christian preaching (Dodd 1944), it seems that once the church moved into the Hellenistic world in the second century a reflective shape became the constant of preaching. Commenting on preaching in the Western tradition in general, Don M. Wardlaw writes: "Preaching, *per se*, has meant marshalling an argument in logical sequence, coordinating and subordinating points by the canons of logic, all in a careful appeal to the reasonable hearer" (1983: 12). For centuries a discursive structure served as a mold into which the sermon content was poured.

The sermon as argument has been the preferred model for most North American preachers in the 20th century. In the 19th century, John Broadus wrote a textbook on preaching that has influenced many contemporary preachers. "Argument," wrote Broadus, "forms a very large and very important element in the materials of preaching.... There are many who deny and doubt who must be convinced of both the truth of Christianity and the truth of what is represented to be its teachings" (1979: 41). Under the influence of teachers like Broadus, preaching has largely entailed a persuasive, logical, orderly way of talking about biblical texts. Hence, after the preacher has determined the message of the text, the classical approach urges her to create an outline which is essentially a schematic diagram of the parts and order of the message.

In support of the traditional strategy of preaching which I have illustrated above, it could be argued that many biblical texts themselves consist of an orderly progression of ideas and some biblical authors, like Luke, describe the preaching of Paul as argumentative in form. Also, congregations have grown to expect rationalistic discourses from their preachers. Admittedly, the sermon as argument has worked over the years; it has been used by God to transform human lives (Stott 1982).

In recent years, however, the validity of this approach to preaching has been called into question. Three assessments are especially common. First, the outline approach to preaching tends to find large concepts or ideas in Scripture that are then divided into categorical points, giving the listener the impression that the gospel itself is simply major concepts with rationally divisible parts. Second, outline-style sermons are static and lack movement because they are artificially constructed with weak transitions that barely join together the various categories of the main idea. Third, it's a method that tends to obscure the real issue of preaching which is not shaping ideas but forming communication so that what is preached is truly heard by the congregation. As Thomas Long says: "A sermon is a plan for the experience of listening, not just an arrangement of data, and it is the listeners who are missing from the typical process of outlining" (1989:96). In recent years the quest for new sermon shapes has been stimulated in part by a growing disenchantment with discursive rhetoric.

 2. The Dynamics of the Human Listening Process. A second reason for the emergence of new sermonic shapes relates to the conviction that sermon form must be controlled both by its biblical content and the dynamics of the human listening process. "What has renewed the question of sermon form among contemporary homileticians is actually the rediscovery, aided by studies in the psychology of human listening, of an old truth: sermon forms are not innocent or neutral" (Long 1989: 97).

 During the past forty years communication theory has abandoned the idea of a passive audience and replaced it with the concept of a highly active, highly selective audience, manipulating rather than being manipulated by a message (Wilbur Schramm 1993: 170). In one sense, preaching has simply been affected by influences at work in the larger culture. Now many preachers are constructing sermons that reflect an awareness of the listener's role in the preaching event. These preachers invite their hearers to share the responsibility for completing the sermon. In this way, the center of authority in preaching has shifted from the preacher toward the listeners.

 Scholars have studied the way language functions, identifying the major modes of discourse and the dominant characteristics of these forms. For example, Amos

Wilder writes: "These are: proximity to oral conversation in that the language is immediate, spontaneous and not discursive in style; the speech is related to the everyday concrete life of the community of faith; and the speech places the listener into the scene, to evoke from him or her some response" (Hobbie 1982:18). In a nutshell, contemporary preachers are creating sermons that are listener-oriented. These sermons are explicitly aimed at involving the listeners. Are these sermons faithful to the character of the Christian message? Well, let's just say that many preachers have joined the choir and are eagerly singing the anthem that listener-oriented sermons are demanded by the rhetoric of the *kerygma* itself (Long 1993: 172).

3. The Fusion of Biblical Form and Content. Biblical scholars have long established the inexorable connection between form and content in Scripture. In fact, the recent revival of interest in sermonic form is in part an attempt to ensure that preaching should be both biblical in form and biblical in content.

Because of the predictable similarity of all traditional sermon forms, the sermon has often been defined pejoratively as "three points and a poem." But preachers are moving away from predictability of form by taking their cue from the great variety of forms in the Bible. For example, Richard Jensen argues: "If the text 'makes its point' in story form then we ought to seriously consider constructing a sermon that is faithful to the content and the form of the biblical text.... Why should we de-story these stories in our sermons and simply pass on the point of the story to our listeners" (1980:128). In similar fashion, Old Testament scholar and preacher Elizabeth Achtemeier writes: "Because the story of God's salvation of humankind is presented to us through the heart-stirring genres of the Bible, it therefore follows that if we are to proclaim that story, we should do so in words and forms that will produce the same telling effects. Why turn God's love into a proposition" (1980:46).

It is now widely acknowledged that meaningful form of any kind participates in the content it embodies. For preachers this means that the sermon's form should work in concert with its content. There should be an integral relationship between the sermon's form and its content, the Word of Scripture. When this happens there is a better chance that the preached Word of Scripture will be heard and felt by today's congregations (Wardlaw 1983: 60). This is not a call for the preacher to slavishly imitate the biblical form, selecting the same literary form for the sermon. "The preacher's task, "explains Thomas Long, "is not to replicate the text but regenerate the impact of some portion of that text" (1989:33-34). In practice the preacher wrestles with an important communication question, namely, How can I shape my sermon to achieve for the contemporary hearer what some aspect of the text wishes to achieve? The literary form of the biblical text may at times serve as a model for the sermon and at other times the preacher will need to select a very different shape in order to be faithful to Scripture.

In short, instead of thinking of sermon form and biblical content as separate realities, it is important to understand that the form of a sermon may undermine the very message of the biblical text upon which the preacher is speaking. Of course, the reverse is also true. The form of the sermon, when appropriately designed, may facilitate the communication of the biblical message as originally intended.

The traditional discursive method tends to view the form of the text only as a vehicle for its content. Once the message or major idea of the text is discerned, the form of the text is discarded. Today new forms are emerging precisely because preachers have been reminded of the inseparable nature of form and content.

Three reasons, then, are often cited for the emergence of new forms in preaching: first the predictability and monotony of the discursive method of preaching; second, the contemporary interest in the dynamics of the human listening process; and third, the conviction that biblical form and sermonic form are inextricably linked.

Hopefully, my reader is now in a better position to consider some of the newer preaching approaches. Think of this book as a travel guide of the current homiletical land-

scape. Here you will find three new sermon forms described in broad strokes, including sermon preparation
tips and a sample sermon by each homiletician. Also, the
theology of preaching that lies behind each approach is
briefly described and each strategy is carefully evaluated
in terms of its strengths and weaknesses. Finally, I will
conclude my discussion of each method by providing a
sermon that implements it in order to demonstrate that
contemporary preachers can adapt these sermon strategies.

As you read, keep in mind that with each approach
there is a demonstrated respect for the diversity of literary
forms in Scripture as well as a concern that the sermon
captures the attention of its listeners. My hope is that one
or more approach will catch your fancy and encourage an
extended stay.

CHAPTER ONE

Craddock's Problem-Solving Strategy

According to Eugene Lowry, a new era in preaching was born when Fred Craddock's book, *As One Without Authority,* was published in 1971 (Lowry 1985:12). Craddock makes a strong case for the inductive method of preaching; he is convinced that the inductive method is a form of preaching that incarnates the message of Christianity. Perhaps the real key to understanding his approach to sermon structure is recognizing that it is a "problem-solving" strategy (Long 1989: 98). Craddock would have the preacher design a sermon in which the people are given all the information they need to solve a specific problem for themselves. It is important, however, to understand that in Craddock's view the problem being solved by the people is the meaning of the biblical text for today. He writes: "It is a call for a program... of biblical preaching that is more realistic and more responsible as far as the bearing of the congregation's situation upon understanding the message of the text" (1971:126). For Craddock the one problem to be solved is the problem of the text's contemporary meaning.

Fred Craddock subscribes to the old dictum that without solid theory, solid practice is not possible. He is persuaded that persons involved in the praxis of preaching must have a clear idea of its underlying principles and theory. Indeed, he argues that effective preaching requires some understanding of its significance, its nature, and its role in the purposes of God. For Craddock preaching cannot be sustained over the long haul by custom or preference alone. It's an error for the preacher to assume that the authority of the biblical text, or the faithful attendance of God's people, or the inspiration of the worship service will alone sustain the pulpit. What's needed is a theoretical framework. "A theology of preaching," says Craddock, "sustains and nourishes the pulpit with a constancy that survives the ebb and flow of the feelings of the one standing in it as well as the smiles and frowns of those who sit before it" (1985:48).

I will now describe Craddock's theology of preaching and provide a sample sermon by him, analyzing it for the reader's benefit. Then I will describe his inductive approach to preaching, organizing my discussion around the five categories of movement, imagination, unity, text, and structure. Next, I will provide a sermon based on the text of Acts 17:16-34 that attempts to implement Craddock's approach. Finally, I will evaluate Craddock's approach in terms of its strengths and weaknesses.

Craddock's Theology of Preaching

Revelation and preaching are distinct yet interrelated modes of communication for Craddock. By definition, preaching makes the revelation of God present to the hearers in an appropriate manner. It is important to observe that he is speaking of the mode of revelation, not its content. He understands revelation to be a certain way of speaking. How one preaches must be harmonious with God's mode of revelation. In a nutshell, the preacher's method of communicating is learned from God. God teaches the preacher how to preach. "The way of God's Word in the world is the way of the sermon in the world" (Craddock 1985:52).

1. Proceeding from Silence. Craddock builds a theology of preaching by means of three biblical images, namely, proceeding from silence, heard in a whisper, and shouted from the rooftop (1985: 51-65). Silence is integral to God's revelation. If the ancient world knew God as silence, the early church proclaimed that God is no longer silent. God has spoken. Jesus of Nazareth is the Word; he is the Word with which God has broken the silence. In this ancient description of Jesus Christ as the Word that broke God's silence, Craddock finds his description of preaching and the sermon. Preaching is characterized as breaking the silence for the sermon is "a word tossed against the clear glass of silence behind which people sit waiting and asking, 'Is there any word from the Lord?'" (1985: 54). The preacher needs to honor silence. Words spoken against a backdrop of silence are more readily heard. Often, the persons who most influence us are those who exhibit a silence that is a quality of their character. For these persons, silence is the context out of which their words and actions flow.

2. Heard in a Whisper. God's revelation is heard in a whisper. Craddock insists that revelation is both about grace and is itself an act of grace. It's an act of grace in the sense that by making himself known in the person of Jesus of Nazareth, God has satisfied the fundamental human appetite, namely, to know him. Yet God's self-disclosure has not been obvious to everyone for God has not broken the silence with a shout but "in a whisper, that is, in ways not all have heard" (1985: 55). God's self-revelation is not so overwhelmingly clear that people are forced into faith by the sheer weight of the evidence. The revelation of God in Jesus occurs somewhere on the spectrum between opaque and transparent. To experience Jesus of Nazareth in the first century was to experience the God who simultaneously reveals and conceals. Mark reminds us that Jesus' disciples did not grasp the significance of his earthly career, especially when he began to speak about his death. After his death Jesus was seen alive again by various followers but among non-believers in and around Jerusalem there is no similar record of seeing the risen Christ. The voice of God in Jesus of Nazareth was not so self-evident that even disinterested and casual passersby were crushed into faith. All of this means that faith is not the end result of tallying up the evidence. Rather, "the believer has leaned forward, heard the whisper, and trusted it to be the voice of God" (1985:57). What preachers need to remember is that not everyone hears a whisper.

3. Shouted from the Rooftop. It would be wrong to conclude that this means that one is to preach in a whisper. At the ear, the Word of God is a whisper; at the mouth, it is a shout. Preachers must reject the deadly idea that since all do not hear, all cannot hear, and hence all are not supposed to hear. Such thinking turns the gospel into a secret, the church into the elite, and Jesus into a riddle. The parable of the soils cannot be used to justify holding tightly to the seed until one has located the good soil that will guarantee a full harvest. We are not called to exercise such careful selectivity. We are called to sow the seed indiscriminately. The earliest church learned that the Word generates a response of trust in Samaritans, Greeks, Ethiopians, and Romans as well as Jews. By "shout" Craddock does not mean the preacher's style of delivery. Rather, he means that what we preach is public proclamation. And to "shout a whisper" means speaking boldly and clearly, trusting the Word as the sower trusts the seed to carry its own future in itself and to make its own way into the heart. It means respecting the listener's resistance to the message, recognizing that resistance is expressed in many forms such as irregularity in attendance and criticism of the petty, always mindful of the fact that both poor preaching and good preaching are hard to hear.

It is important to note that Craddock readily acknowledges the provisional nature of his theology of preaching. As he states: "A theology of preaching is no more than an attempt to discern the way of God's Word in the world and to align one's mode and manner of preaching accordingly" (1985: 65). Ultimately, the preacher of God's Word says: "This is the way I work because of my understanding of the way God works."

Sample Sermon by Craddock

"Praying Through Clenched Teeth" is a sermon by Fred Craddock based on the text of Galatians 1:11-24 (Cox 1981: 47-52). The sermon is reproduced here to illustrate his inductive strategy of preaching. Please read the biblical text of Galatians 1:11-24 in a suitable translation prior to the reading of the sermon.

Sermon
"Praying Through Clenched Teeth"

I am going to say a word, and the moment I say the word I want you to see a face, to recall a face and a name, someone who comes to your mind when I say the word. Are you ready? The word is "bitter." Bitter. Do you see a face? I see a face. I see the face of a farmer in western Oklahoma, riding a mortgaged tractor, burning gasoline purchased on credit, moving across rented land, rearranging the dust. Bitter.

Do you see a face? I see a face of a woman forty-seven years old. She sits out on a hillside, drawn and confused under a green canopy furnished by the mortuary. She is banked on all sides by flowers sprinkled with cards: "You have our condolences." Bitter.

Do you see a face? I see the face of a man who runs a small grocery store. His father ran the store in that neighborhood for twenty years, and he is now in his twelfth year there. The grocery doesn't make much profit, but it keeps the family together. It's a business. There are no customers in the store now, and the grocer stands in the doorway with his apron rolled up around his waist, looking across the street where workmen are completing a supermarket. Bitter.

I see the face of a young couple. They seem to be about nineteen. They are standing in the airport terminal, holding hands so tight their knuckles are white. She's pregnant; he's dressed in military green. They are not talking, just standing and looking at each other. The loudspeaker comes on: "Flight 392 now loading at Gate 22, yellow concourse, all aboard for San Francisco." He slowly moves toward the gate; she stands there alone. Bitter.

Do you see a face? A young minister in a small town, in a cracker box of a house they call a parsonage He lives there with his wife and small child. It's Saturday morning. There is a knock at the door. He answers, and there standing before him on the porch is the chairman of his church board, who is also the president of the local bank, and also the owner of most of the land round about. The man has in his hands a small television. It is an old television, small screen, black and white. It's badly scarred and one of the knobs is off. He says: "My wife and I got one of those new twenty-five-inch color sets, but they didn't want to take this one on a trade, so I just said to myself, 'Well, we'll just give it to the minister. That's probably the reason our ministers don't stay any longer than they do, we don't do enough nice things for them.'" The young minister looks up, tried to smile and say thanks. But I want you to see his face. Bitter.

Will you look at one other face? His name is Saul, Saul of Tarsus. We call him Paul. He was young and intelligent, committed to the traditions of his fathers, strong and zealous for his nation and for his religion, outstripping, he says, all of his classmates in his zeal for his people. While he pursues his own convictions, there develops within the bosom of Judaism a new group called Nazarenes, followers of Jesus. They seemed at first to pose no threat; after all, Judaism had long been broadly liberal and had tolerated within her house of faith a number of groups such as Pharisees and Sadducees and Essenes and Zealots, so why not Nazarenes? As long as they continue in the temple and in the synagogue, there's no problem.

But before long, among these new Christians a different sound is heard. Some of the young radicals are beginning to say that Christianity is not just for the Jews but for anyone who believes in Jesus Christ. Such was the preaching of Stephen and Philip and others: it doesn't really matter if your background is Jewish as long as you trust in God and believe in Jesus Christ. This startling word strikes the ear of young Saul. "What do you mean, it doesn't matter? It does matter! It is the most important matter." No young preacher can stand up and say that thousands of years of mistreatment and exile and burden, of trying to be true to God, of struggling to be his people and keep the candle of faith burning in a dark and pagan world mean nothing. What does he mean, it doesn't matter to have your gabardine spat upon, and to be made fun of because you are different? Of course, it matters!

Imagine yourself the only child of your parents, but when you are seventeen years old, they adopt a seventeen-year-old brother for you. When you are both eighteen, your father says at breakfast one morning: "I have just had the lawyer draw up the papers. I am leaving the family business to our two sons." How do you feel? "This other fellow just got here. He's not really a true son. Where was he when I was mowing the lawn, cleaning the room, trying to pass the ninth grade, and being refused the family car on Friday nights? And now that I'm eighteen, I suddenly have this brother out of nowhere, and he is to share equally?" How would you feel? Would you be saying, "Isn't my father generous?" Not likely.

Then imagine how the young Saul feels. Generations and generations and generations of being the people of God, and now someone in the name of Jesus of Nazareth gets this strange opinion that it doesn't matter anymore, that Jews and Gentiles are alike. You must sense how Saul feels. All your family and national traditions, all that you have ever known and believed, now erased completely from the board? Every moment in school, every belief held dear, every job toward which your life is pointed, now meaningless? Everything that grandfather and father and now you believed, gone? Of course, he resolves to stop it. The dark cloud of his brooding bitterness forms a tornado funnel over that small church, and he strikes it, seeking to end it. In the name of his fathers, in the name of his country, in the name of God, yes.

Now, why does he do this? Why is he so bitter at this announcement of the universal embrace of all people in the name of God? Do you know what I believe? I believe he is bitter and disturbed because he is at war with himself over this very matter. And anyone at war with himself will make casualties even out of friends and loved ones. He is himself uncertain, and it is the uncertain person who becomes a persecutor, until like a wounded animal he lies in the sand near Damascus, waiting for the uplifted stroke of a God whom he thinks he serves.

But Paul knows his is a God who loves all creation. He knows; surely he knows. Saul has read his Bible. He has read that marvelous book of Ruth, in which the ancestress of David is shamelessly presented as a Moabite woman. Certainly, God loves other peoples. He had read the book of Jonah and the expressed love of God for people that Jonah himself does not love. Paul has read the book of Isaiah and the marvelous vision of the house of God into which all nations flow. It is in his Bible. Then what's the problem? His problem is the same problem you and I have had sometimes. It's one thing to know something; it's another thing to know it. He knows it and he does not know it, and the battle that is fought between knowing and really knowing is fierce. I know that the longest trip we ever make is the trip from head to heart, from knowing to knowing, and until that trip is complete, we are in great pain. We might even lash out at others.

Do you know anyone bitter like this; bitter that what they are fighting is what they know is right? Trapped in the impossible battle of trying to stop the inevitable triumph of truth? Do you know any-

one lashing out in criticism and hatred and vio-
lence against a person or against a group that represents the humane and caring and Christian way?
If you do, how do you respond? Hopefully you do
not react to bitterness with bitterness. We certainly have learned that such is a futile and fruitless
endeavor, just as I hope we have learned we do not
fight prejudice with prejudice. A few years ago,
many of us found ourselves more prejudiced
against prejudiced people than the prejudiced people were prejudiced. Then how do we respond?

Let me tell you a story. A family is out for a
drive on a Sunday afternoon. It is a pleasant afternoon, and they relax at a leisurely pace down the
highway. Suddenly the two children begin to beat
their father in the back: "Daddy, Daddy, stop the
car! There's a kitten back there on the side of the
road!" The father says, "So there's a kitten on the
side of the road. We're having a drive." "But Daddy, you must stop and pick it up." "I don't have to
stop and pick it up." "But Daddy, if you don't, it
will die." "Well, then it will have to die. We don't
have room for another animal. We have a zoo already at the house. No more animals." "But Daddy,
are you going to just let it die?" "Be quiet, children;
we're trying to have a pleasant drive." "We never
thought our Daddy would be so mean and cruel as
to let a kitten die." Finally the mother turns to her
husband and says, "Dear, you'll have to stop." He
turns the car around, returns to the spot and pulls
off to the side of the road. "You kids stay in the car.
I'll see about it." He goes out to pick up the little
kitten. The poor creature is just skin and bones,
sore-eyed, and full of fleas; but when he reaches
down to pick it up, with its last bit of energy the kitten bristles, baring tooth and claw, Ssst! He picks
up the kitten by the loose skin at the neck, brings
it over to the car and says, "Don't touch it; it's
probably got leprosy." Back home they go. When
they get to the house the children give the kitten

several baths, about a gallon of warm milk, and intercede: "Can we let it stay in the house just tonight? Tomorrow we'll fix a place in the garage." The father says, "Sure, take my bedroom; the whole house is already a zoo." They fix a comfortable bed, fit for a pharaoh. Several weeks pass. Then one day the father walks in, feels something rub against his leg, looks down, and there is a cat. He reaches down toward the cat, carefully checking to see that no one is watching. When the cat sees his hand, it does not bare its claws and hiss; instead it arches its back to receive a caress. Is that the same cat? Is that the same cat? No. It's not the same as the frightened, hurt, hissing kitten on the side of the road. Of course not! And you know as well as I what makes the difference.

Not too long ago God reached out his hand to bless me and my family. When he did, I looked at his hand; it was covered with scratches. Such is the hand of love, extended to those who are bitter.

Analysis of Craddock's Sermon

A brief analysis of Craddock's sermon, "Praying Through Clenched Teeth," will prepare the way for a consideration of his theory of homiletics in the following section. Several aspects of his sermon are worthy of our attention.

First, the sermon features a series of shifts or transitions between the biblical text and other sermon material. It begins outside the biblical text, with no references to it, and then moves inside the text's story. Thus, the sermon shifts back and forth between the text and other illustrative material. It is a sermon design that alternates the story. But notice that Craddock's sermon makes a limited number of shifts between the biblical text and other material because he does not want to forfeit the attention of his listeners. If the sermon starts outside the text, the first shift into the biblical story happens with the paragraph that begins with the words, "Will you look at one other face. His name is Saul, Saul of Tarsus." After a brief paragraph, he shifts outside the text with the words, "Imagine yourself the only child of your parents, but when you are seventeen years old, they adopt a seventeen year old brother for you." Then after another short paragraph, he shifts back inside the biblical text when he says, "Then imagine how the young Saul feels." Finally, he shifts outside the text, and stays outside the text, with the words, "Do you know anyone bitter like this; bitter that what they are fighting is what they know is right?" A minimum number of shifts between the biblical story and contemporary material are crucial if the preacher wants to retain the interest of his listeners. Too many shifts back and forth makes your listeners feel like they are watching a tennis match!

Second, at the outset of the sermon, Craddock says the word "bitter" and then invites the listener to recall the face of a person that fits the word. But before we can think of a face, he supplies not one, but a series of faces: a farmer, a woman, a man, a young couple, a minister. With great skill, he describes a series of five scenes involving people who have good reason to be bitter. Each scene ends with the word "bitter." In this way, Craddock moves from the particular to the general, from specific experiences to the notion of "bitterness." Also, while the initial scene is a single sentence, each succeeding scene is more developed with the last scene requiring eleven short, crisp, and simple sentences. Why does Craddock begin the sermon outside the text with these five contemporary vignettes? Is he not nurturing our ability to empathize with bitter people and preparing the way for our identification with Paul?

Third, having developed our capacity to empathize with Paul, the sermon then shifts beyond the five opening vignettes and introduces us to Paul by going behind the text to his life prior to his conversion to Christ. In sympathetic tones, Craddock gives us a glimpse of Paul as a loyal and faithful Jew who is upset with young Christian radicals intent on overthrowing everything he values. In this way, Craddock helps us to understand the motives behind Paul's persecution of Christians. Then, leaving the biblical story about Paul's heritage, he develops a family image, comparable to Paul's personal story, that invites us to imagine how a young seventeen year old man would feel if his father were to adopt another son the same age and immediately grant the adopted son full inheritance rights. We would likely be pretty bitter! Finally, he leads back into the biblical story, inviting us to imagine how Paul must have felt when young upstart Christians insisted that what his people have valued for generations doesn't matter anymore. In this way, Paul's bitterness drives him to seek to end this new religious movement before it destroys his people.

Fourth, after all the sermonic effort to explain and to help us identify with Paul's bitterness, Craddock surprises us by asking why Paul is so bitter. In four brief sentences he suggests that Paul's real problem is interior, that is, he is at war with himself. At this point in the sermon we assume that Craddock has reached the climax of his analysis of Paul's problem. Yet he immediately adds another twist: the head to heart struggle common to all of humanity, including Christians. Paul knows in his head that God cares about all people, but it has not yet reached his heart. Indeed, Paul's problem is our problem. As Craddock states, "His problem is the same problem you and I have had sometimes."

Fifth, in the final stages of the sermon, Craddock leaves the biblical text again and shifts to the contemporary scene, inviting us to reflect on our own encounters with people who are bitter. The key question is, how do we respond to bitterness? Then, instead of telling us in explicit terms how to respond to bitter people, he finishes the sermon with a story about a kitten. Of course, we assume that the preacher's story will tell us how to respond to bitterness. As it turns out, it is a story that contains both the indicatives of grace and the imperatives of the gospel—go and do likewise! As a result of the family's love and care, the kitten that once hissed on the roadside becomes a loving family pet. Love made the difference.

By way of conclusion, Craddock closes with a brief but imaginative portrayal of God's hand of love reaching out to bless those who are bitter. And please note the economy of words. Craddock is a firm believer in limiting the number of words we use as preachers since he is convinced that too many words dampen the listener's willingness to hear the sermon.

Craddock's Inductive Method

With his theology of preaching in hand, so to speak, Craddock makes a strong case for inductive preaching. He is convinced that the inductive method is a form of preaching that incarnates the message of Christianity; it is a homiletic form that is well suited to the content of the gospel and the nature of the Christian faith (Craddock 1971: 3-4). I will explore his approach by considering five features that are integral to an inductive sermon, including movement, imagination, unity, text, and structure.

1. Movement of the Sermon. Movement is an important methodological consideration for effective preaching. There are basically two directions in which thought moves: deductive and inductive. The traditional method of deductive preaching presents the thesis first, and then attempts to prove it, explain it, or encourage it, and usually in three points. Deductive movement is from the general truth to the particular application or experience. It is the traditional method of preaching all too familiar to many congregations today. Yet, it is as old as Aristotle.

Craddock is especially critical of the deductive approach on three accounts. First, it assumes an authoritarian foundation for preaching that is no longer appropriate in contemporary North American culture. The movement from general conclusion to particular application is a "most unnatural mode of communication, unless, of course, one presupposes passive listeners who accept the authority of the speaker to state conclusions which he (she) then applies to their faith and life" (Craddock 1971: 23). The deductive sermon may have been appropriate when Christendom prevailed but it is an authoritarian approach to preaching that is inappropriate for a post-modern congregation. There is no democracy with this approach, no dialogue, no contribution by the listener. A different method is needed, a method that avoids the condescending style of the deductive method.

Second, the deductive approach to preaching does not enhance the movement of the sermon. The very structure of a typical three-point sermon is an obstacle to sermonic movement. Often such sermons are little more than three sermonettes barely glued together. There may be some general kinship among points, but there is not one movement from beginning to end. Some preachers have reacted against this deductive pattern instinctively, having sensed that "such a structure violated the experience of communicating and the sense of community to be achieved" (Craddock 1971: 56).

Third, the traditional deductive approach is theologically bankrupt. As a method it contradicts the content of the gospel and the very nature of the Christian faith. As a sermonic form it is defined more by Greek rhetoric than the nature of the Christian faith. "The separation of form and content is fatal for preaching," says Craddock, "for it fails to recognize the theology implicit in the method of communication" (1971, 3). A preacher's hermeneutical principles, his view of the authority of Scripture, church, and pulpit, and especially his doctrine of man, are reflected in his method of communication and the movement of the sermon. "Effective preaching calls for a method consistent with one's theology because the method is the message; form and content are a piece" (Craddock 1971: 20). A perfectly good sermon, content-wise, on the theme of the priesthood of all believers may in effect be contradicted by the method of its presentation if it does not allow the listeners the freedom to respond or give the hearers room to be priests in any responsible sense. What's needed is an alternative method.

In Craddock's opinion, the inductive approach to preaching is a commendable contemporary strategy. Induction moves from the particulars of experience that have a familiar ring in the listener's ear to a general truth or conclusion. This approach has at least two advantages. First, it is an approach to preaching in which the method of proclamation and the method of preparation coincide. In the pulpit on Sunday morning, the preacher simply replicates the inductive movement of thought experienced in his or her study during the week. Second, it is a method that empowers the hearers to apply the conclusion of the sermon to their own lives. "If they have made the trip," argues Craddock, "then it is their conclusion and the implication for their own situation is not only clear but personally inescapable" (1971: 57).

Craddock stresses three aspects of the relationship between inductive movement and the listener. First, concrete experiences common to both the preacher and his/her listeners are integral to the inductive sermon. "Fundamental to the inductive movement are identification with the listener and the creative use of analogy" (Craddock 1971: 59). God's people should recognize the preacher's message or material. The inductive approach recognizes that the congregation is more than just the destination of the sermon.

Second, respect for the capability and the right of the hearers to participate in the movement of the sermon and to arrive at their own conclusion is fundamental to the inductive approach. The movement of a good sermon can be compared to the movement of a good story, a good joke, or even a conversation around a table. The advantage of this type of movement is that "it creates and sustains interest, and it does so by incorporating anticipation" (Craddock 1971: 62-63).

Third, the inductive sermon invites the listener to complete the sermon. Too often the preacher tells the people what they need to do and then they are called to implement his or her applications. The inductive strategy asserts that "the participation of the hearer is essential, not just in the post-benediction implementation, but in the completion of the thought, movement, and decision-making within the sermon itself" (Craddock 1971: 64). This invitation for the hearer to complete the sermon is characteristic of God's way of relating to humans. "One could characterize God," says Craddock, "as reticent to be obvious, to be direct and hence to overwhelm, even when men called for some clear and indisputable evidence from heaven" (1971: 65). While it is difficult to do, especially for preachers obsessed with the need to be certain that their message is heard, the inductive approach calls for incompleteness and a lack of exhaustiveness in the sermon itself.

In my judgment, inductive movement in preaching is meritorious for at least three reasons: first, it corresponds to the way people ordinarily experience reality; second, it respects the hearer and grants the listener the freedom to respond; and third, it sustains interest by means of anticipation.

Integral to Craddock's approach is the assumption that, while exegesis and preaching are not identical, they are, nonetheless, inseparable. They are distinct, yet interrelated activities. The problem at this point for Craddock is that sermons that unhook exegesis and preaching lack unity and movement whereas sermons that exhibit these qualities tend to dispense with either the biblical text or the contemporary situation.

Craddock proposes an alternative method and makes two suggestions in the process. First, he invites the preacher to use the same inductive process in delivery as he used in the preparation of his sermon. In traditional preaching the route from studying the text to structuring the sermon is like ascending a hill (inductive exegesis in the study) and descending a hill (deductive sermonizing in the pulpit) with the congregation experiencing only the deductive side of the journey. While the preacher experiences the thrill of discovery as he ascends the hill by means of inductive study of the text, the people experience no such joy for they must descend, starting with the preacher's conclusion, the summit of his work, and then move deductively to a consideration of the various life-related applications of his thesis. What's wrong is the movement of the sermon. So Craddock proposes that preachers make the method of proclamation the same as the method of preparation.

Second, if movement and unity enroute from exegesis to sermon is to be achieved, the preacher must give greater attention to the place of the congregation. "Giving disciplined time and attention to the interpretation of one's listeners is critical for preaching," argues Craddock

(1985: 98). In reality the preacher does not study the text alone. She studies the text from the perspective of the congregation's situation, bringing the congregation's circumstances to bear upon her understanding of the text and its message for them. This means at least five things: it means dispelling the fear of interpreting Scripture by and for the people, accepting our responsibility to Scripture and for Scripture as members of the church, bearing the burden of facilitating the congregation's hearing of the message of Scripture for their situations, growing the sermon out of a dialogue between a specific text and a specific congregation so that the truth of the sermon is the truth for a specific faith community, and expressing the message of the text in language indigenous to the congregation's circumstances (1985: 126-131).

2. Imagination in Preaching. Craddock readily acknowledges the heavy demand that inductive preaching makes upon the preacher's imagination. If the listeners are to hear the text as the preacher heard it in his study, then the preacher will not be satisfied to reduce his experience to conceptual structures like points, logical sequences, and moral applications. The preacher who desires to reflect what she has experienced in the study will do so by means of images rather than conceptual structures.

Although imagination is crucial to all types of thinking and problem solving, Craddock believes its significance in our day has been reduced by those who associate imagination with fantasy alone. Hope and imagination go together like hand and glove. For example, no thinking person would reduce hope's image of the lion and lamb lying together to fantasy. Images are crucial to the preaching event. "By means of images," argues Craddock, "the preaching occasion will be a re-creation of the way life is experienced now under the Gospel." (1971: 81).

The preacher's imagination is best nurtured not by focusing on the use of imaginative words but by cultivating the preacher's ability to receive images. The preacher must remain alive to the ordinary sights and sounds of life and read quality literature. Getting involved with the life of the congregation also nurtures his capacity for empathetic imagination. "The preacher's task," argues Craddock, "is to use evocative imagery that will allow his congregation to see and hear what he has seen and heard" (1971: 92). And what the preacher has seen and heard is not information about God, but "our existence as it is in the liberating light of God's graciousness towards us" (1971: 92).

Five principles are critical to the function of imagination in preaching. First, images should be drawn from ordinary life and in forms that are real and recognizable. Next, since the force of the sermon depends upon communicating what the hearers will recognize, the preacher's words need to be concrete so they convey what can be heard, seen, smelled, touched or tasted. For example, if the sermon reminds the listeners of the memory of the odor of burped milk on a mother's blouse it evokes more meaning than a critical analysis of motherhood (1971: 93). Third, an economic use of words is crucial. Communication must leave room for discovery. Fourth, avoid all self-conscious interruptions during the sermon. Don't interrupt the sermon with phrases like "we find in this story" or "we see out this window" for they only serve to draw attention to the preacher. Fifth, use the vernacular in the pulpit. These five principles, then, guide the preacher in his capacity to express what has been impressed upon him by life.

Of course, there are many objections to the use of aesthetics in homiletics. Some argue that it fails to contribute to human transformation. Others maintain that it does not appeal to everyone. But preaching's burden is "to share the whole Gospel with the whole person" (1971: 86-90).

3. Unity of the Sermon. If movement is a primary characteristic of effective and persuasive preaching, then unity is essential to that movement. Indeed, Craddock insists: "There can be no movement without unity, without singleness of theme" (1971: 100). Inductive sermons do not have "points," but they do have a single theme that governs the preacher's selection and rejection of material for the sermon. The contribution to the movement and power of the sermon made by the restraint of a single idea cannot be overstated. It's the discipline of this one idea that contributes to the preparation, delivery and reception of the sermon.

During the preparation process, it's the restraint of a single idea that releases the imagination. The theme must be firmly fixed in the preacher's mind as she prepares the sermon. A broad topic has no center of gravity; it draws nothing to itself. But a precise and clear thesis draws potentially helpful material from current and remembered exposures to people and books. With a single idea in mind, the preacher is free to assemble a sermon, excluding what is irrelevant and including what is pertinent to the single germinal idea that is the destination of the sermon. Also, during the delivery of the sermon, the presence of a single theme contributes to the forcefulness with which the sermon is communicated. The presence of a governing theme focuses the energy of the preacher on the unfolding of the single germinal idea that is the point of the sermon. Moreover, while listening to a sermon, the presence of a single focus contributes to interest and meaning. "Unity does for the sermon," says Craddock, "what a frame does for a picture" (1971: 102).

To those who object to the idea of a single-idea sermon, Craddock has three pieces of advice. First, no preacher can say everything at once. Second, a preacher should preach as though there will be a tomorrow. Third, to deal with one problem and/or issue thoroughly each Sunday is better medicine than saying a little about several things. Thus, a sermon's boundaries contribute to its interest.

Admittedly, achieving singleness of theme is difficult, especially for those preachers who take the biblical text seriously. The rich nature of the biblical material seems to be violated by the insistence upon extracting a single theme from it. So how can the preacher say one thing and say it well? First, a thorough exegetical analysis of the text is the only way to discover the governing theme for the sermon. Although the text may contain a cluster of ideas, all those ideas may be subordinate to a larger umbrella theme which can then be treated in a single sermon. Second, the desire to be thorough in one's treatment of a text may lead the preacher to sacrifice unity of theme. But the preacher must take the time to discover the point of the story and allow that point to govern all other considerations. Third, the preacher should guard against the seduction of using the concordance to create a sermon that strings together a cluster of verses on a common theme. He should also resist the seduction of using the easy text that seems to contain a pre-packaged outline like the triad "faith, hope, and love" of I Corinthians 13:13. The preacher should resist any temptation that short-circuits struggling, studying, and wrestling with the biblical text in search of a governing idea that is the key to a forceful sermon (Mohler 1988: 40). Unity will be facilitated best by stating the central germinal idea in one simple affirmative sentence.

Most sermons today exhibit a broken unity with part of the sermon oriented toward the past and the other part toward the present. The primary reason for this lack of unity is the bipolar nature of the task of preaching. Preaching struggles with what the biblical text *said* (yesterday) and what the text *says* (today). Unity is essential to movement in preaching and this unity requires an interpretive approach that bridges the distance between the past and the present with substantial continuity. As Craddock says, "the absence of serious interpretation of the biblical text endangers the Christian character of the sermon while the presence of such biblical interpretation endangers the movement of the sermon and the unity essential to that movement" (1971: 117). How, then, is Scripture to be interpreted so that the unity integral to inductive movement in preaching is supported and the careful exegesis of the text is not endangered?

4. The Biblical Text. Craddock is convinced that the biblical text has a future as well as a past. Preaching brings the Scriptures forward as a living voice in the congregation. He approaches the biblical text on the basis of a cluster of theological convictions about it. First, since the Scriptures are normative for the life of the church, it is suicidal, spiritually speaking, to deprive the church of her life source in preaching. "Sermons not informed and inspired by Scripture are objects dislodged, orphans in the world, without mother or father" (Craddock 1985: 27). Second, since the Scriptures watch over the life of the church, it is self-defeating to preach self-serving sermons for they are called into question by the texts upon which they are based. Third, since a moving text of Scripture that is well read generates expectancy in the listeners, it is foolhardy to preach boring sermons that disappoint God's people.

Serving the futurity of Scripture is a difficult task to be sure. In Craddock's opinion, the following question is the acid test for determining whether the sermon serves the text's futurity: "Does the sermon say and do what the biblical text says and does?" (Craddock 1985: 27). Of course, discerning what the text is saying and doing is no easy matter. He readily acknowledges "historical study only serves to make one more keenly aware of the distance between the text and the present, giving one the distinct impression of moving away from rather than toward the pulpit" (Craddock 1985: 113). However, five favorable factors assure us of the possibility of interpretation. First, our common humanity with the original readers of the text helps to bridge the distance between yesterday and today. Often we can recognize the human condition articulated by the biblical text with a little probing. Second, the interpreter approaches the text with the help of the church's twenty centuries of interpretive tradition. "The image of one person sitting alone with the Bible is unreal and undesirable" (1985: 135). Third, the presence of a community of scholars within the church helps to reduce the gap of understanding between us and the text. All preachers should welcome these colleagues and hear them out before jumping to conclusions about the text's meaning. Fourth, the revealing and interpreting ministry of the Holy Spirit enables the interpreter to narrow the gap between ancient text and today. "It is unreasonable to believe," says Craddock, "that the Holy Spirit was active in the writing and preserving of the canon and then abandoned the church that had to interpret these texts as a living voice to guide believers" (1985: 136). Fifth, the text itself serves to challenge and modify our interpretations of it. Biblical texts have not only survived all our grappling efforts to understand them but they continue to provoke, confirm, and sometimes reject our efforts.

If, as Craddock asserts, biblical preaching moves inductively, how then does the preacher approach the text? How does the preacher foster a dialogue between the congregation and the text? Craddock suggests a procedure with four distinct stages (Craddock: 1986).

a. Getting Into the Text. This stage involves five steps, including selecting the text, reading the text, establishing the text, determining the text's parameters, and contextualizing the text in terms of historical, literary, and theological settings (1985: 99-117). While his treatment of these matters is standard exegetical fare, he does make a number of very helpful suggestions along the way for preachers. For example, allow the text itself to confront the preacher before he is challenged by the wisdom of the commentaries. "It's difficult to get the congregation and text in conversation if half a dozen experts are already at the table" (1971: 134). Second, engage the text by asking it real questions that are opposite to the affirmation of the text. For example, if the text asserts that "all things are yours," is the opposite true that "nothing is yours"? Third, listen carefully to the text to ensure that one receives its message before he shares it with others. Fourth, remember that time spent in study is time spent with God's people in a particular congregation. "They share in what goes on there and will benefit continually from it" (Craddock, 1971: 140).

b. Getting Out of the Text. Assuming that one has been engaged by the text in the process of "getting into it," the interpreter must now disengage or withdraw from the text and recover her distance from it. "No encounter with the text is healthy if either the text or the interpreter loses identity as a center of meaning, decision, and action," says Craddock (1971: 117). In order to withdraw, the interpreter must become self-conscious about his relation to the text for it has a bearing on the sermon soon to be designed. By asking two questions the interpreter can facilitate a greater awareness of her relation to the text. The first question to ask is, "At what level did I engage the text?" In Philippians chapter two Paul quotes a christological hymn of the earliest church and at another level he uses the hymn to instruct the church. Thus, the preacher must decide to preach either christology or Christian conduct based on that christology. The second question that facilitates withdrawing from the text is, "At what point did I identify with the text?" With what character or characters did the preacher identify? If the preacher has been studying Paul's treatment of the role of women in worship in the Corinthian church, he withdraws from the text by becoming conscious of his position in the text. Was he standing next to Paul? Beside the women? Or, in the back of the room contemplating what's going on? Craddock encourages the preacher to be intentional about this matter so that in his interpretation and preaching he is not always taking the best seats in the texts. It's healthy to shift perspectives on occasion.

   c. Arriving at the Message. The preacher now assumes full responsibility for being an interpreter of the text by putting its message into his/her own words. This involves stating what has been heard and experienced in the text and it is best facilitated by answering two key questions. First, what is the text saying? Craddock wants the preacher to state the message of the text in one simple affirmative sentence. "By making the sentence an affirmation one is more likely to capture the Good News than if stated in hortatory terms (we must, we ought, we should, let us, let us not) that too often characterize entire sermons. The exercise of writing a simple affirmative sentence marks an achievement, rewarded not only by a sense of satisfaction but by a new appetite for the next task: the sermon itself" (1971: 122).

   Second, what is the text doing? The text is doing something as well as saying something. Determining what the text is doing is best achieved by attending to the historical and literary contexts as well as the form of the text. What a text does relates to whether the text is correcting, instructing, celebrating, encouraging, or challenging, to mention a few options.

The preacher who has followed Craddock's approach now has something to say and something to do. He has reached what Craddock calls the "Eureka!" point of the sermon preparation process. It is best to engage in some other activity totally different from study and reflection at this point. Indeed, it's important to distinguish the process of arriving at something to say from the subsequent process of finding a strategy that will communicate that content to listeners. The two steps cannot be collapsed into one and for good reasons. First, the interpretive work of arriving at a message must precede the homiletic work of designing a sermon. How can one work at designing a method of communication if the message of the text has not yet been determined? Second, arriving at a message and understanding what the text is doing does not necessarily facilitate the discovery of a design for the sermon. The two processes are distinct, having their own integrity, their own purpose, and their own climaxes. Indeed, Craddock suggests that there are two eurekas, one when the preacher arrives at a message and another when she completes the task of designing the sermon. As Craddock puts it, "Unless the minister has two eurekas, it is not likely the listener will have one" (Craddock 1971: 85).

d. Designing the Sermon. If the preacher has heard the Word of God, how is the message to be proclaimed? What is the form of the sermon? The concern now becomes the fourth stage of sermon preparation. There is no single form that can be designated "the sermon." If anything, the presence of a great variety of literary forms in the Bible calls for a commensurate diversity of sermonic forms. Moreover, the biblical examples indicate that "form itself is active, contributing to what the speaker wishes to say and do, sometimes no less persuasive than the content itself" (Craddock 1985: 172). Form and content are interrelated and interdependent aspects of preaching. Indeed, Craddock insists that "form determines the degree of (listener) participation" (1985: 174). When choosing a form, preachers should select forms that are congenial to the message and the preaching event.

Many preachers are turning to the biblical text itself for

their sermon form and Craddock is quick to encourage this congruence of biblical form and sermon. Indeed, there are several advantages to shaping a sermon in light of the biblical text: first, it ensures variety in form; second, it enhances the integrity of the sermon if both its form and content come from the same source; third, it encourages the preacher to discover the purpose of the biblical form (praise, correction, encouragement, judgment) and to replicate that purpose in her preaching; and fourth, it invites the question, "Will a change of form from the text to sermon alter the meaning of the text for the listener?" (1985: 179). For these reasons, then, there is great value in sermon forms that are rooted in the biblical text itself.

Another method of selecting a form is to go to the storehouse of forms that have been common to speakers and preachers for centuries. Here are a few examples of common forms:

> What is it? What is it worth? How does one get it?
> Explore, explain, apply
> The problem, the solution
> What it is not, what it is
> Either, or
> Both, and
> Promise, fulfillment
> Ambiguity, clarity
> Major premise, minor premise, conclusion
> Not this, nor this, nor this, but this
> The flashback
> From lesser to greater

The value of these forms is that they have proven themselves capable of conveying the truth with clarity and they will guarantee a measure of variety for the listeners. But "no form is so good that it does not eventually become wearisome to both listener and speaker," says Craddock (1985: 177).

A final method is to create a form in accord with the inductive method which demands two things of an outline. First, structure is subordinate to movement in inductive preaching. The preacher's primary concern is making the flow of ideas coherent while concerns about structure are secondary. Structure, which is often not noticeable to the congregation, exists to facilitate sermonic movement. "Usually," suggests Craddock, "for the skeleton to be showing, with a sermon as with a person, is a sign of malformation or malnutrition" (1971: 140). Second, the outline starts with the present experience of the hearers and moves to the point at which the sermon leaves the hearers to make their own decisions and conclusions. "It bears repeating that a preaching event" says Craddock, "is a sharing in the Word, a trip not just a destination and not handing over a conclusion" (1971: 146).

5. Structure of the Sermon. With the above three basic approaches to designing a sermon in mind, the preacher needs to consider several dimensions of the movement of the sermon in relation to structure. First, the preacher begins the preparation of the sermon with the conclusion, not the introduction, for the beginning point of the actual preparation process is knowing where the preacher and the congregation are going. It may even be helpful to write one's conclusion at the bottom of each page of the sermon manuscript. Second, on a sheet of paper, plan the trip to the conclusion in outline form, remembering that it is important to sustain anticipation if all persons and all the faculties of each person are to make the complete journey. To parody Mark 2:27, the outline is made for man, not man for the outline. Third, in the interests of creating an outline that sustains anticipation and hence movement, the preacher can learn much about how to gain the involvement and participation of his hearers by reflecting on poems, essays, and parables that proved effective in his own experience. In any case, effecting the quality of anticipation "is a primary burden of movement in a sermon" (1985: 166).

The very nature of the inductive sermon means there is no single inductive outline or pattern. Still, Craddock does offer several suggestions for those who wish to use inductive movement in preaching. First, since preaching is oral communication, the preacher is advised to prepare his sermon with a view to how it will be preached. "It is reasonable," writes Craddock, "that one operates as much as possible in preparation as one will operate in delivery" (1971: 154-55). Second, it may be helpful to list ideas down the page in brief phrases or sentences in order of occurrence, asking if the material moves and sustains interest to the end. Third, maintain the image of a trip by identifying the transition points in the story and marking them with the appropriate phrases. Fourth, underline the transitional phrases, using them as pegs on which to hang a series of ideas. By noting these transitional expressions, the preacher can readily see the movement of his thought and the shape of his emerging sermon. "The sole purpose is to engage the hearer in the pursuit of an issue or an idea so that he will think his own thoughts and experience his own feelings in the presence of Christ and in the light of the Gospel" (Craddock 1971: 157).

What then does an inductive sermon look like in actual practice? Essentially it consists of a series of movements of ideas and thoughts that build toward a climax. The smaller units of the sermon are linked together by transitional phrases that enable the listener to put the pieces together. All in all, the inductive sermon form focuses on making the flow of ideas coherent so that "it corresponds to the way people ordinarily experience reality and to the way life's problem-solving activity goes on naturally and casually" (1971: 66).

Craddock notes that congregations may experience inductive sermons as one long introduction with an implied message at the end. Hopefully, the people will not shake off the finished sermon as easily as they shake the preacher's hand. "The sermon, not finished yet, lingers beyond the benediction, with conclusions to be reached, decisions to be made, actions taken, and brothers (and sisters) sought while gifts lie waiting at the altar" (1971: 158).

Craddock's Approach Implemented

"The Dance of the Liberated" is a sermon I prepared for a seminary student and faculty retreat early in the academic year of 1995. It is based on the biblical text of Acts 17:16-34 and reproduced here to demonstrate that Craddock's approach is understandable and can be adapted by today's preachers. Please read the biblical text prior to reading the sermon.

Sermon
"The Dance of the Liberated"

One of the questions that hangs in the air around seminary campuses, especially at the beginning of a new academic year, is the question: Why are we here? Why are we in seminary? What am I doing here? What are you doing here? What is the combination of forces and wills, decisions and circumstances that in the mystery of God's providence has led this special group of people to this unique school at this moment in their lives? Why are we here?

We all know that it is not only people on seminary campuses who ask that question, but I do believe that seminary communities face the question in a more pointed way than others. For some reason theological decisions and religious vocational moves demand deeper than usual explanation and justification. For example, tell someone you're going to law school and they say, "Terrific, which one?" Tell someone you're going to medical school and they say, "Wonderful, which one?" But if you tell someone you're going to seminary, they say, "Really, and why is that?"

Ari Goldman is an orthodox Jew who took a year's leave from his job as a religion reporter for the *New York Times* and enrolled in the Harvard Divinity School. He wanted to learn more about the world's religions. Listen to what he says about the seminarians he encountered at Harvard: "I found the Divinity School very refreshing. In an age when most students on college and university campuses are increasingly oriented toward landing good jobs and making oodles of money, I was surrounded by men and women who wanted to pur-

sue the ministry, one of the worst paying profes-
sions" (*The Search for God at Harvard*, 19).

So apart from money, there are many reasons
why we might be here today. Most of us have already been called to justify to someone, somewhere,
why we might be here today. And we all have our
answers. Some of us are here, I suppose, because of
a tug we felt somewhere in our hearts. Although it
did not have a sharp face, nor a clear name, it
seemed like a call to ministry and so we left our
places of work and study, loaded our clothes and
packed our books into the car and we're here.

Others are here become some place of service is
calling us. We have been moved by the plight of
the suffering of the sick and dying, seen the needs
of those in prison, heard the cries of those who are
hungry and homeless, and because of what we
have heard and seen, we put down our nets, left
our boats, and we're here.

Still others are here because we are concerned
about the quality of the church's ministry, because
we are committed, in a landscape of cluttered con-
sumer churches and status-seeking clergy, to the
equipping of pastors who have integrity and a passion for God's redemptive justice and mission in
our world and so, we're here.

There are numerous reasons why you happen
to find yourself in seminary. All of the reasons
make perfectly good sense, or at least enough
sense to place you in seminary rather than some
other place at this point in your life.

Yet I want to suggest this afternoon that there is
a deeper reason for being here. In a sense, none of
our personal stories can quite name the fullness of
why we are here today. We all have our reasons
and we can add them up, but the sum doesn't
equal the total. Ultimately, there is something peculiar, something odd, something outlandish,
something "out of place," about our being here today.

I draw this to your attention today because in the story we read this afternoon from the book of Acts, there is something outlandish, something out-of-place, something peculiar about this picture of Paul standing on the Areopagus, quoting Greek writers in his Hebrew-Christian sermon to an assortment of Philosophy 101 types who are truly curious to find out if this "parrot" knows what he is talking about. In fact, Luke seems to have crafted this story to illustrate the out-of-placeness that characterized the whole ministry of Paul.

Nothing we know about Paul's earlier life can fully account for his being in that place. He was born into a devout Jewish home. He was a citizen of the realm. He had a good education, perhaps both the rabbinical and Hellenistic varieties. Those are the facts. Take that beginning and project it into the future and what do you see? I see a Paul who is a good citizen, active at the local synagogue, maybe even a rabbi. I see Paul at the dinner table with his wife and their children who were growing up like olive shoots, children who would one day ask, "Pappa, why on this night of all nights?" And then old Paul would nod his head wisely and tell the ancient story of the exodus that he knew and loved and lived so well.

But that was not to be Paul's place. No—three times beaten with rods, once pelted with stones, three times shipwrecked, frequent journeys with danger from rivers, danger from robbers, dangers in the city, danger in the wilderness, sleepless nights, hunger, cold, thirst, not to mention the daily anxiety and pressures of life in the ancient near east, including according to Acts, this appearance on a hill in view of the Parthenon, surrounded by Athenians who considered him a propagandist for outlandish gods and who laughed at his deepest convictions. That's the kind of experience that prompts the question, "Why is this person here?"

Well, we know the answer to that question; at

least we think we do. Paul was there in the same way that we are here—because something happened to him. He was changed. He was now alive in Christ in ways that put him where he would otherwise not be. The story of Paul's conversion on the road to Damascus is well known, and surely Paul would say that his transformation on that day made him willing and eager to be in unlikely places.

But I think we need to be careful here. People frequently talk about Paul's conversion experience, but one of the people who does not speak in those terms is Paul himself. When he describes the Damascus Road experience in Galatians 1:11-24, he does so, not in the language of conversion experience, but in the classical language of a prophetic call. In other words, his focus is not primarily on something that bubbled up within him, but rather on a claim that came from outside of him. He talks less about his becoming alive to Christ than he does about Christ becoming alive to him. To be sure, Paul was transformed by the experience, but before he was changed, he was transfixed by the presence of the risen Christ. Even in the Acts account, we do not find Paul gliding away from the Damascus Road experience singing the convert's song of a new orientation, "Amazing grace, how sweet the sound.... Once I was blind but now I see." No, to the contrary, his song could only have been, "Amazing grace, how disturbing the presence... once I could see, but now I am blind."

So may I suggest that Paul stood there that day before the Council of the Areopagus not first and foremost because he had changed, but first and foremost because the world had changed, the new age had dawned, the new age had dawned with the death and resurrection of Jesus Christ, the new age had dawned with the coming of the Spirit of Christ. Paul stood there because the ages had shifted, the old had passed away and the new had come. Paul's ministry occurred along the shifting fault line of two ages, at the churning juncture of the old and the new. Paul was there because of what God had done in Jesus Christ when he raised him from the dead.

So what does this mean for us? Well, it means that we are freed from the compulsion to justify our presence at seminary solely on the basis of our personal devotion, commitment, or knowledge. In fact, when we try to do that, we are always in a fearful and defensive posture. Every new thought, every divergent opinion, every person who does not believe the way we believe, must be viewed as a threat, because if our interior justification for being here should collapse, then the gospel has collapsed for us and we no longer belong in this space. But, as Paul told the Athenians, the good news is that God does not live in shrines made by human hands, not even theological hands, not even the shrines of personal religious experience. On the contrary, it is God who gives everything— everything! It is God who brings life out of death; it is God who causes the old to pass away and the new to come. We do not own the gospel, and we do not have to protect our private understandings or fear the gospel's destruction. We do not even have the gospel; the gospel has us and always comes to us, liberating us to be the people of the risen and living Christ. "With Easter," writes Jurgen Moltmann, "the laughter of the redeemed, the dance of the liberated begins" *(The Church in the Power of the Spirit*, 110).

Friends, Paul was there because of what God has done in Christ and that means that we are liberated from the need to explain our presence at seminary solely by pointing to our personal and interior religious experiences. And it means that we too stand precisely where Paul stood right at the churning and suffering place where the old age grates against the new age, where the laughter of the redeemed is surrounded, as it was in ancient

Athens, by the old era's laughter of scorn; it means that, like Paul, we stand where, in the eyes of the watching world, the dance of the liberated looks a lot like carrying a cross.

A few years ago I traveled to Central America with five other pastor types in order to learn something about God's presence and work among his people in that part of our world. In each country, Guatemala, El Salvador, Nicaragua, and Honduras, we would get off the plane decently and in order, with suitcases loaded down with everything we North Americans think is essential—from bug spray to peanut butter and tums. We soon became embarrassed by all the possessions we had brought and humbled by the awareness that true wealth was not in our suitcases or travelers' checks, but in the joyous faith we encountered in those small congregations we visited in a poor and troubled land. At one point, we confessed to our brothers and sisters in Central America that our time with them was a time of judgment. We publicly acknowledged that we seek our security in so many things, and we mean things—money in the bank, cars on the road, diplomas on the wall, satellites in space. But they rest securely in the arms of God. They know instinctively that nothing is sure but the love of God.

In Nicaragua we expected to be viewed with suspicion as North Americans, especially since the USA was practically at war with Nicaragua at the time. Instead, we were astounded by the many ways in which we were embraced by our brothers and sisters in Christ. We were drawn eagerly into their worship, swaying to the strange rhythms of their joyful hymns and songs, laughing and clapping to the beat of the tambourines with a new-found freedom and joy. So much so, that at one evening worship service that lasted 7 hours, the pastor of the little congregation whispered to one of my traveling companions, "I think the devil is having a real bad time seeing us worship together this way, I think this is a bad day for the devil."

At one point on our trip, we went to a small house in the Nicaraguan countryside where a few members of a little church had gathered for a Bible study. It was just a one room, mud floor house with a few rough benches and a handmade chalkboard. All around there were signs of distress: the poverty of the housing, the signs of war's destruction, a few scrawny chickens running through the yard, and everywhere the haunting faces of hunger. But on the outside door of this house someone had written, in Spanish, the words, "Who lives?" The pastor then opened the door to show us on the inside of the door, written by the same hands, the words, "Jesus Christ lives!"

On the hinges of that door in Nicaragua swings the shifting of the ages. Where are we? In the age of "Who lives?" Why are we here? We are here because "Jesus Christ lives!"

Craddock's Method Evaluated

1. The Strength of Craddock's Method. The first and most notable strength of Craddock's approach is its commitment to biblical preaching. On the occasion of the publication of *Preaching*, Craddock, who is a New Testament scholar by training, was asked to define biblical preaching. He responded by saying: "I think biblical preaching is that form of preaching which gets both the content and the purpose of the message from the text itself" (Mohler 1988: 5). The process of trying to understand the text is critical to biblical preaching. It involves answering the following questions: What is the text trying to do? Is it what I am trying to do? What does the text say? Is it what I am saying?

A second value of Craddock's approach to preaching is the importance it attaches to correlating the rhetoric of the text and the sermon. As one scholar notes, "A hallmark of Craddock's work has been the conviction that the rhetoric of the biblical text and the sermon should complement each other" (O'Day 1993: 11). Leander Keck echoes this praise when he says, "Fred Craddock has been alert not only to the significance of form for understanding the content of the biblical text but also to the role of form in communicating the content of the sermon" (O'Day 1993: 77-78). What's most important to Craddock is that the rhetorical purpose should influence the sermonic form so that the sermon is designed to accomplish what the text's form seeks to achieve (1985: 178).

A third strength of Craddock's inductive method is its emphasis on the value of movement within the sermon. Preaching without movement is a mortal sin in Craddock's opinion. Sermonic movement is what sustains congregational interest in the preached Word.

Fourth, Craddock's approach values the listener's experience. Indeed, for Craddock the listener's experience is the alpha and omega of the preaching event. In one of his most recent works Craddock says, "the goal is not to get something said but to get something heard" (1985: 166).

A final strength of Craddock's strategy is the central place it gives to the congregation. His homiletic strategy has been influenced by his ecclesiology. For example, he insists that the preacher does not study the text alone, or without the people, but rather he studies the biblical text from the perspective of the congregation's situations. Working in the study is time with the people. His approach is clearly listener-oriented.

2. The Weakness of Craddock's Method. Craddock insists that there can be no movement without singleness of theme. He emphasizes the importance of reducing the message of the text to a single affirmative idea that contributes to the preparation, delivery, and reception of a sermon. However, as Richard Eslinger says, "the weak link in his approach is the assumption that the interpretive payoff of every text is a proposition which then becomes the homiletic payoff of every sermonic form" (1987: 125). What happens when the preacher is working with one of Jesus' parables or one of the Johannine signs whose messages simply refuse to be reduced to a single simple affirmative sentence? In such circumstances the preacher's options are limited: either impose a theme upon the text from the outside or sacrifice sermonic unity. For hermeneutical and homiletical reasons, neither option is attractive.

A second weakness of Craddock's inductive strategy concerns its open-ended nature and the role of the listeners in completing the work of the sermon in their reflection and practice. Needless to say, one of the strengths of the inductive approach is that it seems to appeal to the modern mind that has been trained to think everything through and then come to a personally credible conclusion. However, the danger of this open-ended strategy is that people may not know what to do with the message. As Eugene Lowry notes, "It is one thing for a sermon to end in such a fashion that the ball is left finally in the listener's court, and quite another for the ball to evaporate in the drift toward concluding indefiniteness" (O'Day 1993: 111). The limiting factor in this approach is that it demands a creative preacher like Fred Craddock who turns away from the pulpit just when the listeners think there must be at least one more sentence, yet, who, simultaneously, provides the listeners with the kind of clues that enable them to complete the sermon. Fine and good, but if the listeners fail to get the message on their own, has real preaching occurred?

A third weakness relates to the "distance" experienced between the text and the interpreter. Craddock notes that one of the effects of critical biblical methods on preaching is that the preacher becomes aware of the distance between himself and the ancient texts. While Craddock acknowledges that this experience of "distance" is an essential stage in the process of interpreting the text, he wrongly assumes that living with the text serves to overcome the distance encountered. Some biblical forms like apocalyptic, miracles and signs, and the resurrection and ascension narratives seem to be highly resistant to decreasing the "distance" in spite of the exegetical skills of the interpreter.

A fourth weakness of Craddock's strategy relates to its reduced teaching value. At least one of preaching's purposes in the church is teaching. Perhaps James W. Cox is right when he says, "I believe that it would be impossible to do a thorough job of consecutive Bible exposition or give a good account of the Bible's teaching without going at our task much of the time deductively" (1990: 64). We can safely assume that a large part of every congregation will already be predisposed to accept the Bible and Christian teaching as true in one way or another. If so, it is our responsibility to show how it is or may be true for them in thought and life and service. Not everyone who hears us needs to be teased into hearing the word of God.

A final weakness of Craddock's approach to preaching is a theology of preaching that centers more on preaching's method to the neglect of preaching's content and motive. One could argue that what we preach and why we preach is as important, if not more important, than how we preach? In a recent interview with Albert Mohler, Craddock was asked, "Why do we preach?" He responded by saying: "Well, because we must. We must join the biblical word with the human voice of the believer standing up in the company of other believers. Preaching has a socializing, community-building force. It brings the page of the text to life in an oral way. The nuances of the human voice maximize the content of the biblical message" (1988: 4). Yet in his brief theology of preaching Craddock chooses to stress the mode of God's revelation. In the process, little attention is given to the content of preaching. Also, when drawing our attention to the Christian sources that treat God's silence, he mentions Ignatius' presupposition that God was silent before he sent Jesus Christ. Craddock attaches value to silence itself. Now it's true, that in the ancient Hellenistic world, silence was valued and respected. In fact, "Silence" was a symbol of the highest deity. God was "Silence" because he was understood to be utterly removed; he did not speak; he was a hidden God. It is likely against this backdrop that John's Gospel designates Jesus Christ as "the Logos." In a world that knew God's silence as an attribute of his essence, the Christian message rings out: God is no longer silent—he speaks. What Ignatius and John's Gospel are valuing is not silence *per se*, but the fact that God is no longer silent or hidden. He has spoken distinctly and clearly in Jesus Christ. In Jesus of Nazareth, God has removed his mask. Indeed, Jesus Christ is the Word with which God has broken the silence. All of this does not support Craddock's thesis that "God's silence is integral to God's revelation." What's integral to a Christian understanding of revelation is that God is not silent. Indeed, in Jesus of Nazareth God has spoken for Jesus is the Word with which God has broken the silence.

CHAPTER TWO

Lowry's Suspense-Driven Strategy

Eugene Lowry proposes a narrative strategy for preaching. In Eslinger's opinion, it is a method that "demands the attention and study of every serious proclaimer of the Word" (1987: 65). The term "plot" is the key to unlocking Lowry's reshaped image of the sermon. Although plot formation may vary from sermon to sermon, the glue of ambiguity is the one form that Lowry considers indispensable to the sermon event. He imports narrative theory as the paradigm for developing a sermon with five sequential movements. He provides us with what one homiletician has described as "a fluid, suspense-driven master form for sermons" (Long 1989: 100).

A careful consideration of Lowry's homiletic method makes it apparent that, by the phrase "narrative sermon," Lowry does not mean "story sermon," but rather a sermon that employs the narrative sequence of opening conflict, escalation, reversal, and proleptic closure. For Lowry the term "narrative" refers, not to content, but to form. Indeed, in a recent book Lowry writes:

> I happen to be one of those writers who believe in narrative preaching. That is, I see every sermon as an event-in-time, which moves from opening disequilibrium through escalation of conflict to surprising reversal to closing denouement (1989: 25).

I will describe Eugene's Lowry's theology of preaching, paying special attention to his understanding of the goal of preaching. I will also provide a sample sermon by him that illustrates a sermon imaged as narrative time and then analyze his sermon for the reader's benefit. Next, I will summarize his suspense-driven method, attending in particular to Lowry's five sequential stages of upsetting the equilibrium, analyzing the discrepancy, disclosing the clue to resolution, experiencing the gospel, and anticipating the consequences. Finally, I will provide a sermon that implements his narrative strategy and an evaluation of the strengths and weaknesses of his narrative method.

Lowry's Theology of Preaching

Given the vital role of preaching in Christian ministry, it is odd that there is no consensus on the primary goal of preaching. What's even more intriguing, in Lowry's opinion, is that differences of opinion about the goal of preaching are not based on theological orientation or homiletical tradition. In Lowry's view there are two polar extremes with each one having sermonic goals based on an unconscious image of the sermon. Specifically, one group, for whom the bottom line is understanding, gives priority to ordering ideas, and the other group, for whom the bottom line is some kind of happening, gives priority to ordering experience. Given these two options, Lowry opts for happening. He states his thesis: "A sermon is an ordered form of moving time" (1985: 8). He laments the unconscious influence of the image of ordering ideas which has frustrated the best intentions of preachers who would prefer to operate with a model of ordering experience. Although recent homiletical history has affirmed the ordering of ideas model, Lowry notes "when we do well in the pulpit often it is when we lay aside our outlines of space and begin talking to our people in time" (1985: 27).

Having defined a sermon as an "event-in-time," Lowry explores the question of time. If it can be assumed, reasons Lowry, that time is the characteristic mode of our experience, then the sermon must exist within time, not space. The preacher who opts for ordering ideas into "timeless truths" tends to stop the clock, leaving the sermon hanging in space. By contrast, the preacher who chooses to order experience stays in touch with his listeners who hear in time.

So what does Lowry mean by "time?" There are several kinds of time. He notes that the Hebrew Christian tradition, while rejecting the cyclical conception of time espoused by the Greeks, views time as linear so that it has a beginning and moves toward a definite goal. Linear time is durative and objective, it is time "out there," and Lowry labels it *chronos* time. However, we cannot reduce our experience of time to simply *chronos* or outward time, observes Lowry. In addition, there is subjective time or inward time by which we experience duration subjectively. When a sermon is preached, notes Lowry, "there are as many inner clocks as there are listeners—all ticking at different speeds" (1985: 32). Next, there is *kairos* time, meaning the "right time." Rather than viewing *kairos* as a third kind of time, Lowry sees it as an event in time which implodes two or three other kinds of time. He explains:

> Typically, *kairos* (1) involves an interaction among an exterior event, one's inner time, and chronological time; (2) includes the sense of duration being temporarily suspended (even unselfconsciousness about time's passing); and (3) results in some type of profound impact" (1985: 32-33).

For Lowry, *kairos* is stimulated by story in both theatrical and liturgical settings. For example, when the biblical story of salvation is reenacted in worship, the participants relive it and experience the right time, *kairos*. This last observation raises an interesting question about the connection between *kairos* and God's activity in time. Is it to be presumed that *kairos* and providence are to be considered synonymous terms? Since *kairos* is often used to describe a moment of insight or a season of celebration quite apart from God's intervention, its usage does not always include an assumption about God's activity. Lowry proposes that the faith community should use the term "God's time" when it wishes to point to events-in-time that it perceives to be revelational and providential.

He explains how these various understandings of time relate to preaching. He is persuaded that preaching announces God's time and God's time transforms *chronos* time. Indeed, Lowry believes the goal of every sermon is to effect transformation, that is, "to prompt such intersection of God's time with our *chronos* and inner times that the *kairotic* event happens" (1985: 35). Therefore, as preachers, if we wish to prompt the *kairotic* moment of revelation, we had better begin doing time in the pulpit.

Since he believes that the homiletical vehicle for "doing time" is narrative, he introduces a final aspect of time. For Lowry narrative time begins the moment the preacher enters the pulpit and looks at the people. He writes:

> Picking up *chronos* and inner, reaching for story, announcing God's time and praying for *kairos*, narrative time dances in, through, and around all the times. In one sense measurable by *chronos* but never overcome by it, and intending to transform it, narrative time...is the sermon (1985: 37).

To help us understand the sermon as narrative time, Lowry explores the common dimensions of story including setting, plot, character, tone, and finally, the dimension of narrative time which is peculiar to his view of the sermon. Here it is adequate to note that the sermon, for Lowry, aims to prompt a *kairos* time by bringing *The Story* into relationship with the congregation's various times. Although it is an awesome thought, Lowry hopes that the sermon as event-in-time may "become an occasion when God's time breaks into human history" (1985: 64).

If the sermon is to become a transforming event in time, if the good news is to be experienced through the event of preaching, then, according to Lowry, the focus of our preaching must be upon God's activity. This is the crucial emphasis in Lowry's theology of preaching. The focus of the sermon must not be upon what we do. While our human response to the proclamation of the gospel is important, it must not be the climax or center of gravity of the sermon. The gospel of Jesus Christ must occupy center stage in our preaching if people are to be released from the inevitability of doing evil and set free for loving others even as they love themselves. Lowry writes:

The proclamation of the gospel must be other

than a weekly 'guilt trip' placed upon our parishioners. The awfulness of human guilt needs redemption, not a lecture. The preached Word makes possible the redemption into new life by its announcement of what God has done and is doing (1980:72).

For Lowry, then, the sermon aims to foster human transformation in time by focusing on God's gracious activity in Jesus Christ.

Sample Sermon by Lowry

"Who Could Ask for Anything More?" (1989: 115-121) is a sermon by Eugene Lowry based on the text of Matthew 20:1-16. It is reproduced here to illustrate his suspense-driven strategy of preaching. Please read the biblical text in a suitable translation before reading the sermon.

Sermon
"Who Could Ask for Anything More?"

It was about a quarter of seven in the morning when the owner of the vineyard went to the marketplace to hire workers for the day. They all agreed on a denarius for the day's labor—a reasonable amount. So they went to work. About a quarter till nine, the owner was back at the marketplace—the equivalent of a town square. Finding others were looking for work, the owner said, "Whatever is right I will pay you," and they went to work. About a quarter till twelve, the owner is back at the marketplace—and one wonders why he didn't hire all he needed the first time. Perhaps a storm was coming. And they too go to work. Again, about a quarter till three he's back again— and once more at quarter till five—when there's only one hour of work left.

Now it's six o'clock—time to be paid. The owner whispers (I think) in the ear of the financial steward of the corporation to pay the last ones first. And they have to be surprised. They have worked only one hour—yet they receive a full denarius. They are ecstatic—but not half as much as those who came at seven. "You mean he's going to pay one denarius for each hour's work? Why, that's almost a half month's salary for us." They can't believe it, but they do—until the steward begins paying those who came at three. There's some mistake here. They're getting the same amount. Surely the owner will whisper in the steward's ear again, correcting the mistake.

But he doesn't, and by this time the steward is paying the twelve o'clock folks—and still giving each just one denarius. Smiles have faded from seven o'clock faces. "You mean he is going to pay everybody the same amount, regardless of how much work?" Unbelievable—really unthinkable.

Sure enough, those who came at seven receive just one denarius. The text says they "grumbled"—surely a modest way to put it. (Probably couldn't print what they really said.) "What do you mean, paying us the same as all the rest? Why, those last folks hardly had time to work up a sweat, yet you make them equal to those who have borne the burden of the day and the scorching noontime heat."

"Now, wait a minute, here," the owner responds. "Why should you expect any more? Don't I remember a conversation we had about a quarter till seven this morning? Didn't you agree to work for a denarius?" "Well, yes, of course, but it's all different now, when we see you pay those others the same. Of course, we expect more." "What's the matter—you begrudge my generosity? I choose to pay them the same. I take it that's my business, isn't it? It's my money. You—take your denarius, and get out of here."

Well, I must say—I think they've got a point, don't you? I mean, imagine you came to work at seven—how do you feel just now? What's right here has to do with relative justice, among all the

workers. And the truth is, if you are a public em-
ployer, indeed you do not have a right to "do as
you please" with your money.

So you're on the school board in your town,
about to hire a couple of new teachers. Both have
the same fine college records, same experience.
One male, the other female. You plan to pay the
woman less because of the conditions of the job
market? You'd better not. Somebody's going to be
breathing down your neck, and they ought to be.
Going to hire a couple of folks to do some yard
work—one white, the other black? Same experience. Going to pay the black person less because
you can get away with it? Well, it's wrong.

This story is the same kind of issue, just in different form. I say, this is a good case for the National Labor Relations Board, don't you think? In fact,
I'm shocked. Why on earth would Jesus take the
side of an unjust owner? In fact, you know, that
business of paying the last ones first...that was cruel—and it was dumb. He forced the seven o'clock
folks to watch while the injustice was being perpe-
trated. He'd been a whole lot better off to pay the
seven o'clock folks first—get them out of his hair—
then nine, then twelve. Nobody would ever know.
Besides what's going to happen to the owner tomorrow morning? He's going to go down to the marketplace about quarter till seven—and guess what?
Nobody's there. He'd better come back about a quarter till five—lots of folks there then, ready for work.

There must be something peculiar going on in
this story; otherwise, I just don't understand. Well,
yes, there is, and our first clue was the scene of the
last one's paid first. But you really can't get the gist
of the story unless you go back one chapter in
Matthew.

Remember the scene? Jesus is having a conversation with the one we have come to call the rich
young ruler, who seems to have his life in order except for one thing. Jesus says, "Go, sell everything,

and give it all to the poor—and then come back."

Well, the disciples are listening to this encounter, and they can't believe their ears. They have just returned from a church growth seminar and cannot believe that Jesus would let such an outstanding prospect get away. Jesus sees their shock and says, "I tell you, it is easier for a camel to get through the eye of a needle than a rich man to get into the kingdom." And don't try to demythologize the image here—with the eye representing the gate in the city. No, Jesus means exactly what he says: It is easier for a big fat camel—humps and all—to get through the eye of a little needle than for a rich person to get into the kingdom.

"Well, it's impossible," they say, and they are certainly on target here. Jesus gives them the good news: "Well, with people it is impossible, but with God, all things are possible." But they miss it altogether, and Simon Peter comes waltzing up, one foot in his mouth, and says, "But Jesus, we have left everything to follow you—what do we get?" Hear it? "We've left everything to follow you—what do we get?"

And the answer? Cheated. That's what you get. The kingdom is not a business deal, not a contract, but a covenant. If you start asking, "What's the bottom line for me?" the answer is simple: cheated.

And this "bottom-line" mentality has troubled the church ever since. I remember as a child in a small Methodist church in Wichita, Kansas, listening in on the old folks' conversation. One such conversation went like this: "You know...it's just not fair. You mean to tell me that we who have been faithful to the church, given our money and time, always lived the straight and narrow—you mean to tell me that when we get to heaven, we'll be joined there by that guy who's always done whatever he wanted, really lived it up, until his deathbed conversion experience? You mean the same heaven? Just isn't fair."

Sometimes the attitude comes in tragic form. You're at an area-wide church leadership training event on a Sunday afternoon. They divide you up into small groups and direct you to the proper room and a circle of chairs. Most of the folks you don't know. So the leader says, "Suppose we start by going around the circle and introduce ourselves. Just tell us who you are." You go around the circle until you come to this older man who says, "My name is...and I used to be a plumber." "Used to be?" What does he mean used to be? You hear it? Life is a contract, and his contract ran out. He used to be a person, brought home the bacon. But now, he is a "used to be."

You keep going around the circle until you come to this woman, who looks up sheepishly and says, "Well, I'm just a housewife." Just? What does that mean? It means that she doesn't bring home the bacon either. Now, she has to cook it and clean up after it, and all the rest of an eighteen-hour day, but the contract is a bit fuzzy, you know. "I'm just a housewife."

Now, I want to ask you to imagine that today you are the parent of three children—three, six, and nine years of age. Now, do you love the nine-year-old three times as much as the three-year-old, because, of course, the eldest has been three times as much help around the house? You, who are nine years old—do you love your parents three times as much as you did when you were three? "Why," you say, "that's ridiculous. We're family." Exactly. This is family. So's the story. Jesus was talking about a family covenant. Simon thought it was a business deal.

And do you know where that vineyard owner is this very minute? Why, he's back at the market-place, looking to see if there is anyone else who has not yet heard the invitation, not yet had the chance to respond.

So you see, it doesn't really matter whether the

invitation comes at seven, or nine, or noon, or three, or five, or two till.

To be invited into the vineyard is to be invited home.

Who could ask for anything more?

Analysis of Lowry's Sermon

Lowry generally works with four narrative sermon design options: a) running the story, b) delaying the story, c) suspending the story, or d) alternating the story. The sermon entitled "Who Could Ask for Anything More?" is an example of "suspending the story." The sermon begins by unpacking the parable of the vineyard workers until a problem emerges at which point the treatment of the parable is suspended while another story, in this instance the story of the rich young ruler of Matthew 19, is used to provide a solution to the problem posed by the parable. After the solution to the problem is presented, the sermon moves back to the exposition of the parable of Matthew 20. Hence, Lowry's sermon is a good example of the narrative design called "suspending the story."

Second, the sermon begins inside the biblical text with only a few minor editorial remarks that update the parable for the sake of Lowry's contemporary listeners. As the time of payment for labor rendered arrives, Lowry adds a series of imaginative details like the owner's whisper into the ear of the financial steward, the surprise response of the latecomers who receive far more than anticipated, and the seven o'clock folks who cannot believe the "mistake" that is being made. When the mistake is not corrected, the seven o'clock workers begin to think the unthinkable—the owner is going to pay everyone the same amount! In this way, Lowry builds a case for the sense of injustice about to be experienced by the seven o'clock workers. And when it happens, Lowry steps outside the text and announces that they "grumbled." He gets his listener's back into the text by means of a short dialogue between the seven o'clock workers and the owner of the vineyard. The owner's question ("Why should you expect any more?") to them seems to have a twofold function: it recalls the sermon title and summarizes the seven o'clock worker's argument. Finally, the story reaches its climax when the owner announces his right to be generous.

Third, having narrated the biblical story of Matthew 20, Lowry analyzes the problem that has emerged. He steps aside and invites his listeners to decide for or against the owner. Indeed, he addresses his listeners for the first time by means of the personal pronoun "you." Then he moves away from the biblical story with two contemporary workplace scenarios where we all know there is no room for unequal pay on the basis of gender or racial differences. Finally, he brings the analysis of the problem to its logical conclusion with a piece of humor about the difficulty of trying to hire folk at seven o'clock the next day for work in the vineyard. A significant degree of ambiguity has now been achieved.

Fourth, Lowry then begins to resolve the problem by suspending the story of the workers in the vineyard and by inviting his listeners to consider another story, the story of the rich young ruler of the previous chapter. Notice Lowry's technique of putting one foot inside the biblical story and another outside the story, giving him the freedom to make editorial remarks like his reference to Peter "waltzing up, one foot in his mouth." The response of the disciples to Jesus' demand of the rich young ruler enables Lowry to emphasize the logical conclusion of viewing the kingdom of God in terms of a business transaction. It leads to a "bottom-line" mentality and the feeling of being cheated. At this point Lowry moves away from the Bible to a contemporary story about some old folks talking about the injustice of God's reception of latecomers to the kingdom of God. It helps his listeners identify with the injustice of our story when viewed through contractual eyes. Finally, he relates the contractual view with its emphasis on work as paid employment to the tragic attitudes it breeds in many people at the point of retirement when the contract ends and how it affects the homemaker who does not have a contract and hence does not "bring home the bacon." In this way, Lowry probes the larger implications of the biblical story.

Fifth, by means of a family image, Lowry invites each

listener to imagine that he is a parent who loves his nine-year-old child more than his three-year-old. Of course, it is an absurd scenario. It's ridiculous because Jesus was talking about a family covenant, not a business deal. At this point in the sermon, Lowry introduces the sermonic reversal. While the workplace operates on the basis of the ethic of justice, the home operates on the basis of the ethic of grace. Likewise, the family of God functions on the basis of the generosity of God. In a final imagined scene, Lowry reenters the story with the owner passing by the marketplace, inviting others to respond to his grace and generosity. The clincher comes with the sentence: "To be invited into the vineyard is to be invited home. Who could ask for anything more?"

Lowry's Narrative Approach

For Lowry a sermon, by definition, "is a plot... which has as its key ingredient a sensed discrepancy, a homiletical bind" (1980: 15). If a plot is the moving suspense of story, the sermon, when viewed from the perspective of narrative time, takes the form of moving suspense. Thus, the sermon will have the shape of any given plot.

There are basically two forms of plot: the unknown and the known. Lowry uses the movie "High Noon" to illustrate the first of the plot-forms. The movie begins with a felt discrepancy and moves to an unknown resolution. One is hooked into the felt discrepancy and left wondering, anxiously, how the plot is to be resolved. A second kind of plot moves toward a known resolution. The hero is placed in an impossible situation in which there seems to be no way he can survive. But we know the "hero" will find a solution because he must be back next week for another TV show. This plot-form is common to detective series. The viewer sees the crime and knows the person will be caught. The "bind" comes in figuring out how the detective will discover what the viewer already knows. This type of plot-form involves an unknown middle. In fact, according to Lowry, sermons usually involve this second kind of plot. The listeners know the story will end with Jesus alive and resurrected and hence they know the answers to the "bind." Thus, the sermonic development focuses on the unknown middle, giving the sermon tension and discrepancy.

Lowry sets forth a profile of a sermonic plot, noting that it comprises five basic movements or "stages" which function almost like an outline for a sermon. "Because a sermon is an event-in-time," says Lowry, "a process and not a collection of parts, it is helpful to think of sequence rather than structure" (1980: 25). The five basic sequential stages to a typical sermonic process are: (1) upsetting the equilibrium; (2) analyzing the discrepancy; (3) disclosing the clue to resolution; (4) experiencing the gospel; and (5) anticipating the consequences. Lowry suggests that his students remember these steps by means of the following abbreviations: (1) Oops; (2) Ugh; (3) Aha; (4) Whee; (5) Yeah.

1. Upsetting the equilibrium. In the opening stage, the preacher poses the problem of the sermon in a manner that engages the listeners. Within the first two or three minutes, interest must be stimulated, and it is best achieved by upsetting the equilibrium of the listeners. Ambiguity rouses interest because as human beings we have a common felt need to resolve it. Indeed, Lowry believes that the primary purpose of sermon introductions is to produce imbalance for the sake of engagement. For Lowry ambiguity and its resolution is a basic form-ingredient of a sermon. "There is always one major discrepancy, bind, or problem which is the issue," says Lowry. "The central task of any sermon, therefore, is the resolution of that particular central ambiguity" (1980: 31). The strategy of upsetting the equilibrium of the listeners is comparable in function to the opening scene of a movie or play in which tension or conflict is introduced. "Likewise," says Lowry, "a sermon introduction may upset the equilibrium of members of a congregation by means of an inconsequential ambiguity which serves simply to stimulate interest in the sermonic process" (1980: 31).

Lowry offers several suggestions to the preacher intent on triggering ambiguity in the listener's minds and hearts. First, if the introduction involves an ambiguity that is not actually related to the central plot, the preacher must be careful that it does not occupy the listener's attention at the expense of their focus on the central plot of the sermon. Second, it is often the case that the opening ambiguity will be the central discrepancy, especially in sermons addressing the contemporary situation and in sermons that are expositional or doctrinal. For Lowry, the objective is to trigger, not simply intellectual ambiguity, but also an existentially felt ambiguity. Third, while establishing disequilibrium is the key to beginning the sermon, the next step is to keep it and not let it slip away in the next few moments of the sermon. Fourth, although the resolution of the plot is left hanging and incomplete in the first stage of the sermon, direction to the ambiguity must be given. Without disclosing the clue to its resolution, the listeners need to know the plot's direction. While the specific problem and its difficulty is clear, what generates interest at this stage of the sermon is the lack of resolution. In other words, the underlying factor is the suspense created in the listeners because they do not know how the issue will be resolved. Thus, the first step in a preached sermon is to upset the equilibrium.

   2. Analyzing the Discrepancy. Once the opening bind of the sermon has been disclosed and the listeners have been thrown into disequilibrium, the preacher begins the second stage of the sermonic process which involves the task of probing the problem. At this stage the preacher diagnoses the discrepancy or problem, and asks, why? For Lowry this diagnostic stage is not only the lengthiest of the five, often an amount of time equivalent to the other stages combined, but also, for two reasons it is the most critical stage. First, since the sermon seeks to resolve a problem, discrepancy, or bind, the analysis of the discrepancy determines the shape of the sermon as well as the good news proclaimed. Lowry's strategy assumes a correlation between the human problem and the gospel's response. The effectiveness of the cure prescribed to resolve the human dilemma or bind depends on the accuracy of the diagnosis. Second, this stage is for Lowry the primary vehicle for the maintenance of the sermonic plot. At this stage the preacher seeks to create the kind of suspense experienced while reading a good detective story that leaves you wondering who did it. The desire to learn the villain's identity propels the reader forward. "Likewise the suspense of not yet knowing why things are as they are... provides the homilist the opportunity of diagnostic wrestling —of theologizing" (1980: 38).

Regrettably, laments Lowry, preachers often opt for description or illustration instead of diagnosis. He believes that what is missing is depth—a probing into the causative ingredients responsible for the situation. Diagnosis or analysis is what is needed—not description or illustration. Lowry uses the example of a sermon on apathy that calls for a diagnosis of apathy's causes. If a hearer discovers, while listening to a sermon on apathy, that fear of rejection may be a cause of his apathy, then the gospel will speak to the hearer because the good news of God's acceptance reduces his fear of rejection by others. In this way, Lowry argues, "the purpose of the sermonic process of analysis is to uncover the areas of interior motivation where the problem is generated, and hence expose the motivational setting toward which any cure will need to be directed" (1980: 40). Lowry insists that the sermon must treat not only the behavioral level but also the more complicated motivational level. To illustrate his point, Lowry notes that in the story of the prodigal son, the text does not raise the issue of why he left home so the preacher is free to imagine the motives for his departure. Perhaps a negative experience with his older brother coupled with a desire to see the world prompted his leave. The point is that the preacher cannot rest content with mere analysis of human behavior; he must go behind the simplicity of behavior to the complexity of causality.

During the preparatory stage prior to the sermon, the actual process of diagnosis/analysis is easier to state than effect. Ultimately, the preacher must repeatedly ask why the discrepancy/bind/problem exists until he or she reaches the revelatory "Aha" stage. Since Lowry's approach assumes a correlation between the human condition and the gospel's response, the need for in-depth analysis is critical. "When this analysis is superficial, the gospel as proclaimed must of necessity feel like a 'pat answer'; it will lack credibility" (1980: 43).

Also, concerning the actual sermon stage, it is important for the preacher to go through the process of analysis inductively with the congregation in a fairly complete, though modified fashion. The same principle is operative in such a sermon as in the detective story where, although the author already knows who did it, the reader experiences the drama of discovery by repeatedly asking, "Who did it?" In the sermon itself the process of analysis moves the listeners through numerous dead-end routes until the decisive clue is disclosed. If the clue to resolution (stage three) is to be existentially real, and if the gospel is to be heard (stage four), this stage must be prepared by the ambiguity explicit in the analysis of the discrepancy. "The purpose, then, for stage two is not simply for a resolution to be reached but also for a readiness for resolution to be developed" (1980: 45).

3. *Disclosing the Clue to Resolution*. Working with the assumption that we live in a cause-effect world, the ultimate goal of the problem-solving process is to provide the so-called "missing link" or an explanation that accounts for the problem. For Lowry, when the explanation is found and disclosed, it functions as the bridge from problem to solution, from itch to scratch, and enables the listeners to view the problem from a fresh perspective.

Also, characteristic of the problem-solving process is the encounter with numerous "dead-end" solutions that must be discarded so that one can press on toward the real solution which, once discovered, is, in gestalt terms, the "aha," the missing piece that puts the puzzle into proper focus. Lowry says: "Such a revelatory clue is experienced by the congregation rather than simply known" (1980: 48).

Peculiar to the homiletical revelatory clue is the fact that it comes as a surprise; it's not exactly what one anticipated; it turns things upside down; it's what Lowry calls the principle of reversal. "The process of reversal as presented in a sermon," says Lowry, "can be likened to the action of pulling the rug out from under someone" (1980: 56). Of course, the preacher must first lay the rug before he pulls it. Then, with the rug well laid, it is reversal time. While the principle of reversal seems to characterize Jesus' parables, it is found elsewhere in Scripture as for example in the story of Abraham's sacrifice of Isaac where God's command to sacrifice Isaac was really a seemingly nonsensical command for Abraham to destroy the only logical means God had for fulfilling his promise to Abraham. However, Lowry believes that the principle of reversal is more than a literary device. It is rooted in the gospel for there is something about the gospel, which is a reversal of the world's way of viewing truth. "The fundamental mistake of the liberal Protestant pulpit of the last forty years," says Lowry, "is that it presumes that the gospel is continuous with human experience" (1980: 60). However, such continuity is only the case after the gospel has reversed human experience by turning it upside down.

Lowry envisions a sermon that starts by making contact with the members of a congregation at the point of their human predicament (stage one). It then moves through an inductive analysis of the predicament (stage two) to disclosing the clue to the resolution of the issue (stage three) by means of some kind of reversal thereby setting the stage for the proclamation of the Gospel.

4. Experiencing the Gospel. The listener's readiness to experience the gospel is dependent upon the depth of analysis achieved in the two previous stages. Regrettably, an attitude of impatience may lead to an improper diagnosis and cause what Lowry calls a "homiletical short circuit" which is "a giant and ill-fated leap from the beginning of stage two (analysis) to stage five—which is the stage of anticipating what can or ought to be done in light of the intersection of problem and proclamation of the gospel" (1980: 62-63). For example, the issue of one's identity, an illustration Lowry uses, can be short-circuited if the preacher assumes that it is incumbent upon us to search for self and proceeds to offer suggestions in the sermon on how God's people might find their identity. However, it is a false assumption for it seeks to find what can only be given, argues Lowry. "Instead, the gospel declares that we have been found—that identity is a gift one can never obtain or reach on the basis of human effort" (1980: 63).

Another critical factor is the matter of sermonic timing. With respect to the above illustration for example, it would be fatal, homiletically speaking, to announce this good news at the beginning of the sermon. On the other hand, when the context has been properly set in stages one, two and three, when the congregation experiences the utter futility of the search for identity, then the gospel will be proclaimed effectively and credibly, i.e., the gospel does what it says. Of course, Lowry reminds us that the content of the gospel proclaimed in stage four must fit the diagnosis of stage three. "The cure must match the disease," says Lowry (1980: 64). It is not difficult to determine what the gospel has to say to a clearly and deeply diagnosed issue. Indeed, Lowry says: "When I have done my diagnostic homework and the decisive clue has emerged, the good news has fallen into place sermonically as though pulled by a magnet" (1980: 65).

Again, with Lowry's strategy the sermon begins inductively, moves toward the clue to resolution, revealing dead-ends along the way and turning things upside down, and then it proclaims the gospel deductively. Once the gospel has been proclaimed, the homilist is ready to ask about the matter of consequences.

5. Anticipating the Consequences. Stage five explicates the future in light of the good news experienced in stage four. "Plot-wise," says Lowry, "it is the stage of effecting closure" (1980: 67). Essentially the preacher asks what can be anticipated in light of the gospel's intersection with the human condition. The sermon as homiletical plot is different in two important respects when compared with the more traditional sermon construction. First, the traditional sermon reaches its climax in the conclusion's invitation or call to commitment, whereas the sermon as homiletic plot reaches its climax in the resolution stage where everything is turned upside down and viewed in a fresh light. The perception of apparent similarity between the two types of sermons is related to the fact that the final stage of the homiletical plot sermon, anticipating the consequences, is in the same position time-wise as the call to commitment of the traditional sermon. The second difference is manifestly theological. When traditional preaching makes the invitation for a human response the climax of the sermon, it is guilty of works righteousness for it puts the focus on us rather than on God's activity. "To make the call to commitment the central focus of the sermon is to place ourselves in the limelight, where we have no business being," says Lowry (1980: 69). Instead, Lowry says: "The focus of our preaching is upon the decisive activity of God, not upon us, and hence the climax of any sermon must be stage four—the experiencing of the gospel" (1980: 69). While human response is critical, it is not the center of gravity for the sermon. The center is the good news of the gospel of Jesus Christ. The preacher is able to call for a response at stage five only because the gospel has affected a new freedom to choose. Freedom is a consequence of the grace of God. This is a truth illustrated so very well in the story of the woman of Mark 14:1-10. The gospel of Jesus of Christ proclaimed generates the ability to respond.

In sum, Lowry's "suspense-driven" strategy consists of five sequential stages of upsetting the disequilibrium, analyzing the discrepancy, disclosing the clue to resolution, experiencing the gospel, and anticipating the consequences. Since Lowry's narrative plot form is designed to translate any sermon, whether topical, life situational, doctrinal or expositional, into a narrative event, it is important to ask if there is room for variation within the five stage sequence?

While some modification in the five stages of the sermon process may be needed on occasion, "there is one essential form," says Lowry, "which I believe indispensable to the sermon event, and that one essential is ambiguity" (1980: 76). For Lowry variations on the above five-step process may be made as long as the glue of ambiguity is preserved. The major exception occurs when preaching a biblical narrative sermon for the biblical narrative has its own plot and its own ambiguity needing resolution. It does not need another plot line superimposed on top of it. Other variations are also possible. Sometimes the anticipated consequences to the narrative plot may be unstated or only hinted. At other times, for example a funeral sermon, the opening stage of the sermon may be omitted. On still other occasions long drawn out diagnostic analysis may be inappropriate. Yet the most suitable way of achieving variety according to Lowry is by altering the form of the discrepancy from "why" to "how" or "when" or "where." However, for Lowry, "whatever kinds of variation are utilized in the plot formation of a sermon, the glue of appropriate ambiguity is necessary" (1980: 80).

Having explored the five stages of a sermonic plot, it is appropriate to ask at this point, how does one go about the task of preparing a narrative sermon? Lowry devotes considerable space to the subject of preparing a narrative sermon. Indeed, his book, *How To Preach A Parable*, is a "how-to" volume designed to help preachers prepare narrative sermons (Lowry 1989). What motivates Lowry's significant attention to the matter of preparing narrative sermons is the notion that "only the rare and gifted preacher can preach narrative sermons." Of course, Lowry rejects the idea and boldly asserts that "narrative preaching is not an esoteric art form reserved for the few. All of us can utilize the method—indeed, I believe, ought to" (1989: 13).

Preparing the Narrative Sermon

Here I will consider several aspects of Lowry's treatment of the task of preparing a narrative sermon including: suggestions for the preliminary stage of sermon preparation, pointers in telling a story, implications of viewing the sermon as an event-in-time, understanding the properties of a story, and creativity and sermon preparation.

1. Preliminary Preparation Steps. Lowry identifies two preliminary and difficult stages of sermon preparation. First, there is the stage of "wandering thoughtfulness." As the preacher contemplates Sunday's sermon he or she notes potential ideas, reads the lectionary texts, pulls out previously prepared long-range sermon planning notes, and checks the denominational calendar. "At best this stage is one of imagination," says Lowry; "at worst it is the stage of anxiety" (1989: 17). Second, there is the preliminary matter of settling on a sermonic idea. When completed, says Lowry, "this stage represents a transition to a very peculiar state of knowing implicitly that a sermon can happen" (1980: 17). Since Lowry believes the sermon is a narrative plot, the sermonic idea emerges at the intersection between problem (itch) and solution (scratch). He suggests that we begin this preliminary preparation stage by choosing one of these two poles as a starting point and then moving thoughtfully in the opposite direction until the discrepancy or bind is known and felt.

According to Lowry, the following steps are instrumental in giving birth to a sermonic idea. (1) Select a source like a biblical text, congregational need, or ethical issue. (2) Identify the material as problematic, solutional, or resolutional. (3) Press the problem or solution into more specificity by considering its opposite. (4) Experience the bind or discrepancy at the intersection point between problem and solution or when a "problematic itch" intersects with a "solutional scratch" the sermonic idea is born. (5) Set the material within the five stage sermonic plot pattern explicated above (1980: 63).

For example, Lowry selects a text, namely, Romans 7:24: "Wretched man that I am! Who will deliver me from this body of death?" He identifies it as a "problematic itch" for it contains Paul's confession of his inability to do good. Next, he begins moving in the direction of a "solutional scratch" born of the gospel by asking questions about the issues raised by the text. Eventually, his preliminary musings lead him to recognize and feel a discrepant bind between Romans 7:24 and Philippians 4:13 ["I can do all things in him who strengthens me"] by simply observing that both texts are by the same person. How could Paul the Christian make both statements? At this point, Lowry senses, intuitively of course, that a sermon is in its embryonic stage; he feels the bind. What began as two texts, one problematic and one solutional, has emerged as two texts that are problematic by virtue of their contradictory relationship to each other (1980: 81-82).

2. Biblical Narrative Sermons. For Lowry the question

of sermonic form is the central issue in the preparation of a biblical narrative sermon. However, before the several options of sermonic design can be considered, there are several preliminary steps that lead to its choice. There are three major moments or preparation tasks, namely, focus, turn, and aim. These three major tasks assume that the preacher has spent time listening to the text since it is imperative that the preacher hear the text. Also, the three tasks assume that the preacher will avoid the trap of turning to the commentaries too quickly. He urges preachers to read the text aloud, repeatedly in different translations and paraphrases, including the original if possible. At this point it is most helpful to look for trouble, asking what in the text does not fit or what is strange about the text? "Trouble in, around, with, and about the text is often the occasion for a fresh hearing," says Lowry (1989: 33). The three tasks further assume that once the text's trouble, issue or problem has been discerned, the preacher will pursue the problem like an investigator by doing word studies, consulting introductions to the book in commentaries, comparing parallel or conflicting passages and drawing on all the available resources for thorough exegesis.

As the above investigation proceeds, the preacher heads in the direction of the first of three major moments in the preliminary sermon preparation process. The first major task is to ask the question, what is the focus of the text? That is, what is at stake here, what are the issues that need to be addressed? One begins with this question because the narrative approach assumes that the sermon will begin with a problem, discrepancy, a conflict, or an ambiguity that needs resolution. The second major task is to ask, what is the sermon's fundamental turn? This question originates with Lowry's understanding of the narrative form. "Plots should never end quite as expected," says Lowry, "and hence there is a natural anticipation on the part of the listener about the decisive turn that will make all things new" (1989: 34). Although one may not be able to identify the turn within the text at this early stage, we need only to note that somewhere it must appear. So the preacher will be searching for the turn as he continues his investigation of the text. "Indeed, where the turn occurs," writes Lowry, "will help determine which narrative sermon model the preacher chooses" (1989: 34). The last major moment or task in the preliminary preparation of a narrative sermon is determining its aim. What does the preacher hope will happen as a direct result of the sermon's actual proclamation? Admittedly, this determination comes somewhat late in the sermon preparation process.

It's important to note that Lowry encourages pursuing the matters of focus, turn, and aim instead of the common approach of settling on a sermonic theme and boiling it down to a single affirmative sentence. The traditional theme sentence is usually recommended because it serves a useful function in providing precision of the homiletical purpose. However, theme sentences suffer in two respects, claims Lowry. First, they tend to propositionalize the sermon, narrowing the sermonic goal to educational aims such as clarification, amplification, application, and information. Second, they do not stimulate the listener's mind because they encourage the preacher to preach deductively once the theme sentence is stated. For these reasons Lowry prefers to achieve homiletical precision by drawing our attention to focus and aim rather than theme (1989: 35-37).

For Lowry the preparation process begins with the text's problem explored, the text's focus named, and the text's aim sensed. Now the question of the sermonic form becomes the central issue for the preacher who seeks to implement Lowry's narrative method.

There are four options available to the preacher intent on designing a narrative sermon. Lowry identifies the first option as "running the story." It essentially consists of following the flow of the biblical story provided by the text. Although the preacher does such things as highlight and elaborate specific portions of the text, the shape of the text determines the shape of the sermon. Lowry calls it "running the story." The second option Lowry identifies as "delaying the story." Here the biblical text does not immediately appear in the sermon; its entrance is delayed for a variety of reasons. Sometimes the biblical text resolves the sermonic issue. At other times its entrance is delayed in order to deal with a current congregational concern. At still other times it makes its entrance later in the sermon simply because the text is so well known. A third option Lowry calls "suspending the story." With this option the biblical story encounters a problem like an enigmatic statement made by Jesus and thus the biblical story line is temporarily suspended while the preacher moves away from it to a contemporary illustration in order to find a solution to the trouble in the text. Whether the preacher does a flashback to a previous section of the biblical narrative or a flash-forward, or a flash-out, the technique of temporarily leaving the central biblical text in the middle of the story line will be called suspending the story. The fourth narrative design option Lowry identifies as "alternating the story." Here the biblical story line is divided into sections with other kinds of materials placed around the biblical story. Thus, the preacher alternates the telling of the biblical story with relating other material that illumines the biblical story. "When alternating the story design is used well," says Lowry, "it is both a fascinating and a powerful form of narrative preaching" (see 1989: 42-170).

Lowry provides additional preparation help for those preparing to preach on a biblical narrative by drawing on the insights of the art of storytelling. For Lowry the following suggestions, which pertain to the preparation and delivery phases of preaching, are "pointers in telling a story." These pointers include the following twelve items: (1) Attend to every seemingly insignificant detail. The tendency to attend to what is familiar will fail to provide a fresh view. Thus, noting seemingly insignificant details like the older brother's conversation with the servant in the story of the prodigal son may provide an important twist for re-telling the story. (2) Look between the lines. Often the cultural context lying behind the text informs the preacher of a unique feature in the story as is the case when the person who queried Jesus about paying taxes to Caesar only to expose the fact that he was in the wrong place (temple area) with a Roman coin. (3) Catch every encounter. Since biblical narratives move rather quickly, Lowry encourages the preacher to pause between actions to note implicit action as for example in the story of Zacchaeus, the preacher might ask what Zacchaeus may have thought and felt when Jesus addressed him while he was up a tree. Or the preacher might ask how Zacchaeus got out of the tree. (4) Bring data from your own experience. For example, if considering the story of the prodigal son, why not enter the story with some empathy by asking yourself if you ever left home for good reasons or by recalling your own disgust with special treatment doled out to the undeserving. (5) Move behind behavior to motive. Here Lowry suggests that the preacher can help the listeners identify with the story by probing causative factors and by establishing a credible context for hearing the gospel. (6) Move behind facts to prior dynamics. Noting that facts sometimes distort experiential reality, Lowry suggests that examining the underlying dynamics may shift contradictions to the level of ambiguity as in the case of Jesus' question of the man at the pool of Bethsaida ["Do you want to be healed?"] may suggest that Jesus perceived more than the facts warranted, namely, that the man had grown accustomed to his physical condition and really did not want to cope with the lifestyle changes that physical healing would inevitably entail. (7) Utilize the senses. The listener's capacity to participate in the story is greatly facilitated by utilizing the senses as Jesus did in stories like the prodigal son where we are able to hear the music, see the dancing, and smell the food cooking. (8) Switch identification. Biblical narratives should be experienced in such a way that the hurt and disappointment are included as in the case of the five foolish virgins who were excluded from the wedding celebration is experienced as well as the joy of the five wise virgins who were prepared for the event. (9) Utilize active grammar. Noting that passive and subjunctive verbs as well as prepositional phrases destroy the life of oral speech, Lowry suggests using active verbs and strong nouns like biblical narrative employs as in the story of Jonah: "the fish ... vomited out Jonah on the dry land." (10) Break into first and second person singular form. For example, in the story of the prodigal son, while Jesus could have used the third person singular ["the son decided to return home, confess his sin, and ask for a job"] he instead used the first person singular ["I will arise and go to my father, and I will say...."]. (11) Move from the subjective to the objective, from particular to general—and back again. In addition to the details the storyteller must not exclude the bigger picture like the traveler who related the minute details of leaving a hotel room for a tour of the city but failed to relate either the hotel's name or the name of the city or for that matter the overall importance of the experience. (12) Set the stage (foreshadowing). The storyteller alerts the listener to the importance of a later event by foreshadowing it with an early yet unrecognized clue (see 1989: 89-95).

3. Ordering Experience. If the sermon is to become an event-in-time, Lowry believes it will require a paradigmatic shift in thinking about sermon preparation; it will demand a radical shift in thinking that moves from ordering ideas to ordering experience. Most preachers tend to think space rather than time when it comes to sermon preparation. As a result they set about ordering ideas when preparing a sermon. Instead, Lowry invites us to image a sermon as ordering experience. The change in perspective will focus our attention on the congregation rather than a piece of paper in front of us. "Knowing their existence in time (actually several times), we now perceive our work as doing something with their twenty minutes of listening time" (1985: 13). What will arrest their "times" is not ideational content but a story. Such an approach involves action, movement, and duration—elements of time. "A moving sermon," argues Lowry, "is more like a trip that takes us from here to there through the medium of time—from then to now" (1985: 13). For Lowry the compass readings for this trip are taken from biblical narratives, in particular Jesus' teaching strategy which seems to order experience in time rather than ideas in space. However, as persons preparing sermons, preachers need to be aware of the full implications of this shift in focus from ordering of ideas to ordering experiences. Indeed, the paradigm shift encompasses several major considerations which Lowry presents as a series of contrasts between the ordering of ideas and the ordering of experience.

The first is the difference between the task of organizing and shaping. In traditional preaching the preacher is advised to identify a main thesis and then organize subsidiary points under the main point with a view to achieving unity of thought and focus. However, this approach suffers in several respects. One problem is that disunity characterizes most traditionally prepared sermons. "One speaks of attaining unity," says Lowry, "only when one assumes it is not already there" (1985: 14-15). Indeed, often a typical traditional sermon is several complete ideas barely glued together. Another problem is a lack of sermonic movement. The desperate parts of the traditional sermon are complete thoughts. "There is nothing that can close down attention more easily," notes Lowry, "than a complete thought" (1985: 15). An even larger problem with the image of ordering ideas is that it assumes the preacher has mastered the biblical material rather than being called into question and challenged by it. As he says: "One gets the truth in place, declares it, puts it into a proposition. Putty in one's hands" (1985: 15). But Scripture confronts us. It is we who need figuring out, not the Bible. Thus, instead of controlling and organizing, Lowry invites the preacher to listen and to shape experience by attending to movement rather than thought. When shaping a sermon early in the preparation stage, one does not figure out its central message, organize the whole and then fill in the details. Rather, with the congregation's future experience of the sermon in mind, one starts by focusing on a specific portion of the text and by asking small, concrete questions. "The point is," writes Lowry, "work with the specific ingredients of experience allows a more open-ended process of preparation" (1985: 17). Thus, the preacher's task is to shape experience, not organize ideas.

A second difference between ordering ideas and ordering experience while preparing a sermon relates to the form of the sermon. If one's task is to organize ideas the result will be a sermon form that is a structure. But if one's task is to shape experience, then sermonic form will be a process. One way to note the difference is by comparing the sermon notes for organizing ideas with those for shaping experience. The former moves vertically, resembling a building blueprint, while the latter moves horizontally and looks more like a road map. "A sermon process moves in a more linear fashion because life is experienced in time" (1985: 17). Another way to state the difference is by considering the grammar of the central points. With a sermonic structure the key points are declarative propositions that convey finality, whereas with a sermonic process the central points are questions and transition markers that function like road signs guiding one to the destination. Finally, in a sermonic structure, the points are often interchangeable, whereas in a sermon imaged as process the markers are like road signs that cannot be changed without altering meaning.

A third difference between ordering ideas and ordering experience in the preparation stage relates to sermonic focus. The preacher organizing ideas into a structured form will invariably focus on a theme and seek to discover a unifying ideational thread. While a preacher shaping experience into a process form will focus on events and, as Buechner testifies, if there is a theme "it emerges through the events that take place and the interaction of the characters" (Lowry 1985: 19).

A fourth difference between ordering ideas and ordering experience in the preparation of a sermon relates to an important preparation principle. While doing the work of preparing a sermon, the preacher unconsciously evaluates his progress. If the preacher has learned to image the sermon as ordering ideas, then the yardstick for assessing progress will be substance, that is, "Are you getting it said?" Substance as the underlying principle of sermonic evaluation assumes that God's revelation in Scripture is essentially propositional in form. Yet even those who subscribe to a non-propositional view of revelation seem to utilize the principle of substance. "It means," says Lowry, "that homiletical theory has drawn heavily upon the principles of rhetoric and unwittingly borrowed a principle that is not altogether suitable for our task" (1985: 21). By contrast, if a preacher images the sermon as ordering experience, the measuring stick will be resolution, that is, "Are you getting there?" However, Lowry cautions that "narrative trips are different from car trips in that often resolution increasingly becomes more remote and difficult, apparently, until by some strange shift or move the resolution happens with utter surprise" (1985: 21).

A fifth contrast between ordering ideas and ordering experience has to do with the final product of the preparation stage. "If the preacher is ordering ideas, the resultant structural form likely will be an outline," writes Lowry. "If the preacher is ordering experience the resultant process form is plot" (1985: 22). The outline fits the informational image of preaching it represents. Whereas there is some kind of sequential ordering in a plot including, "an opening conflict, escalation or complication, a watershed experience (generally involving a reversal) and a denouement" (1985: 23).

A sixth difference between ordering ideas and ordering experience in preparation relates to the means by which the preacher produces an outline or a plot. An outline is generally acceptable to those who seek to order ideas if it makes sense and communicates the central theme with clarity. What's critical is cognitive coherence. By contrast, an effective plot-like sermonic product exploits ambiguity and suspense. The critical question, argues Lowry, will be "whether ambiguity based on discrepancy is maintained successfully until the preacher is ready to resolve matters with the gospel" (1985: 24). With plot the focus is not on the test of coherence but the test of correspondence. Does the ambiguity and/or suspense maintained by the preacher resonate as real as the listeners experience life?

A final contrast between ordering ideas and ordering experience in preparation relates to the goal of the sermon. Understanding is the bottom line for those who image the sermon as ordering ideas. By contrast, some kind of happening is the critical issue for those who image the sermon as ordering experience. For Lowry a sermon is an event-in-time, and hence, he opts for happening.

Recognizing that a radical shift in sermon preparation from ordering ideas to ordering experience will not occur without a "push," Lowry believes that an appropriation of the power of story provides it.

4. Understanding Story. Since the power of a story resides in its properties of setting, character, action, plot, and tone, Lowry explores these elements together with a sixth that he labels "narrative time."

Lowry begins by considering the element of setting, the first critical property of story with implications for preaching narrative sermons. The role of setting in story is to locate life in space and time thereby providing the hearer with the larger context from which to view the details and specifics. Its location in space and time enables a story to overcome the "abstract-concrete" polarity peculiar to verbal address. Also, setting sets limits to life in the sense that the story's characters are presented as finite, conditioned by time, space and circumstances and hence, recognizable to the listener who shares the finitude characteristic of real people who do not always receive what they need or desire. Lowry laments the fact that much pulpit work announces the victory in Christ before it has adequately identified the human dilemma. But if the sermonic form is narrative, the element of story is a gift for "there is little way we can duck the borders of existence because the negative atmosphere of setting will of necessity provide them" (1985: 46).

A second property of story with implications for preaching narrative is character. Although the expression "human potential" needs to be used with care, the character(s) inserted into the story's setting will reflect the potential of human consciousness to know and manage the world in which it finds itself. That is, the story will summon from the character(s) the powers of decision, growth, accomplishment, and sacrifice. Lowry suggests that what "character in narrative has the peculiar power to do is to sharpen perception about how to think." The conscious paradigm presented by means of the character puts us in touch with our own unconscious image of human potential. As we move through a story, "we are grasped by a new vision of life we never understood before" (1985: 49).

A third feature of story with ramifications for preaching narrative is action. Once the stage is set and the characters have been introduced, events occur that impact the lives of the characters who respond internally and externally to one another. For example, Lowry illustrates his point with a snapshot of a narrative sermon on Zacchaeus:

Jesus is walking into and among the crowd, looks up at Zacchaeus in the tree, and invites him down. Zacchaeus promptly falls out of the tree, brushes himself off, and leads the way to his house. While they walk—presumably at a normal pace—Zacchaeus' thoughts are racing back and forth, while the thoughts of the crowd are doing a slow burn. The parade was a flop, but Zacchaeus' future is new (1985: 51-52).

In this way, a chain of events is created in which action is followed by response which in turn is followed by new action. Something is always happening. But something larger is also going on and Lowry calls it "plot."

A fourth property of story which effects narrative preaching is plot. As noted earlier, plot for Lowry is the moving suspense of story, from disequilibrium to resolution. Its typical stages are (1) opening disequilibrium, gaining complication toward (2) escalated ambiguity, climaxing into (3) reversal, and moving out into (4) denouement. It is the plot of a typical story and for Lowry it is the shape of a narrative sermon.

A final element of story with implications for preaching narrative sermons is tone. For Lowry tone refers to "the work's created subjective presence—the world view that stands silently articulate behind the writing" (1985: 59). It also has to do with point of view which can be the point of view of character, narrator, audience, author, or preacher.

The peculiar elements of story put together include setting, character, action, plot, and tone. Of course, for Lowry, all the elements exist in time. Time is the critical element because the story is bracketed within a time frame, the author depends upon the vehicle of time. And time, says Lowry, "is central because it takes time to hear the sermon, attend the play, read the book. This I call narrative time" (1985: 61).

5. *Sermon Creativity.* Recognizing that a narrative sermon requires some creativity on the part of the preacher, Lowry addresses the question of how preachers can be more creative in their sermon preparation. Three convictions govern Lowry's suggestions on creativity in sermon preparation: first, creativity is not something a few people possess, but rather a potential result we all possess to some degree; second, although one cannot choose to be creative, one can choose the behavioral patterns that stimulate creativity; third, "the key to creativity lies in releasing the creative preconscious mind from the controls of routine consciousness" (1985: 98).

Lowry encourages preachers to behave in a certain way in order to be more creative during their sermon preparation time. First, he advises alternating work with other activities. Creativity is most likely to be released after one has experienced the hard work of focused, intensive, and conscious deliberation of the problem and/or issue of the text quite apart from any consultation of the exegetical experts and without reaching any conclusions about its resolve. Then it's time to let go and do something entirely different. "The purpose of all this is to allow the subconscious or preconscious to go to work on the impasse, unhampered by conscious control" (1985: 99-100). A critical resolution or clue or important missing variable will strike while doing something quite different from actual sermon preparation. Lowry believes the alteration between work and rest maximizes its release. Second, Lowry urges preachers to prepare sermons by talking to oneself, with another person, by role playing, and by using free association. During the early stage of the gestation period of sermonic preparation, creativity often receives assistance by talking the sermonic ideas out loud either with or without another person present. Lowry even suggests having a kind of role playing dialogue with the characters in the text. Third, the most important factor, says Lowry, is to begin writing a sermon before you think you are ready. Here Lowry is following the lead of narrative artists who speak of allowing the story to lead them toward the plot. Finally, Lowry urges preachers to work over their head so that they can work under their head. That is, often the best sermon is the one over which a preacher struggled the most during the preparation time. As Lowry writes:

> … maximizing creativity requires that we get in over our own heads, where the complexity of life leaves us dizzy and the gospel none too neat and tidy. Then we will be drawn into that bind that requires conscious effort and necessary time for preconscious mulling and sorting. Then that quality called creativity has its chance to emerge (1985: 106).

Lowry's Approach Implemented

"If Only You Recognized God's Gift" is a sermon based on the text of John 5:1-16 and preached in the Mennonite Brethren Biblical Seminary chapel in 1998. It is reproduced here to demonstrate that Lowry's approach is understandable and adaptable by today's preachers. Please read the biblical text in some suitable translation prior to the reading of the sermon.

Sermon
"If Only You Recognized God's Gift"

The NIV translation of today's text calls this story "The Healing at the Pool." But notice that our text is not describing your typical California poolside party—you know, fit bodies, great food, cold drinks and fun in the sun. No, the pool in our story is really a local sickbay for people with twisted limbs and paralyzed bodies. These folks are simply trying to cope. There's no party going on here.

Oh, there's a party going on in Jerusalem. The religious folk are whopping it up in the Holy City. It's one of those annual feasts—you know, lots of food, wine, and laughter. But these folk at the pool near the Sheep Gate get no closer to the festivities than the sight, sound & smell of sheep on their way to slaughter—food for the party.

The text does not say why these people are gathered around the pool. But some ancient manuscripts tell us that they were waiting for a miracle. There was a legend about this pool. Once upon a time an angel agitated the water and the first person to get into the pool was healed. Ever since, people in need of healing gathered at this pool, waiting & hoping for the angel to show up once more.

False hope, that's what the legend gave them, false hope! Imagine all the false starts and cold plunges on days when brisk winds gave the effect of an angel's visit. And suppose an angel did stir the water, whom do you think would be the first to get into the pool? The paralyzed and severally crippled? Not a chance! The fittest would win the race into the pool. Clearly, these people lying around the pool are victims of a cruel religious myth.

We can understand, can't we? We all know how easy it is to gather people to a site where a miracle happened, once upon a time. All the shrines and holy places of our world are testimonies to this reality. Right here in California there's a place called St. Joseph's Hill of Hope. Apparently, Joseph appeared one day and revealed where water could be found—a big need in California. Ever since, people from around the world show up, hoping for another miracle. Well, the pool of Bethesda was also a sort of shrine. The people who gathered there were victims of a cruel myth.

One day Jesus shows up. He's on his way to the feast. As he passes by the pool, he notices all the lame people gathered by the water's edge. He stops, and stares at them, catching sight of their rags, taking in their twisted limbs. Dozens, maybe even hundreds of invalids—the blind, crippled, paralyzed and lame—lying around the pool. It's a pathetic sight!

The text says that Jesus fixes his gaze on one man who has been paralyzed for a very long time—thirty-eight years! Jesus approaches him and asks: "Do you want to be healed?"

The man's response is a bit surprising, to say the least. Instead of answering, "Yes, I want to be healed," he complains about the injustice of a system that has all these years kept him from entering the pool first. He grumbles about the young whippersnappers who outrace him into the pool. "Sir," he says, "when the water is stirred, I don't have anybody to put me into the pool. Before I can get into it, somebody else gets in ahead of me." Obviously, this man doesn't know who is speaking to him. If only he recognized God's gift!

Jesus takes no offense. He gives a healing command: "Get up! Take your bedroll, and start walking!" The man was healed on the spot. He got up and walked off, carrying his mat. He went and joined the party. What a wonderful sight!

Well, no, it isn't, at least, not for the religious folk celebrating in the temple. You see, it's a Sabbath day and when they catch sight of the man, carrying his bedroll, they stop him and accuse him of violating a holy day: "You can't carry your bedroll around like that; it's against rules."

Against the rules! After 38 years as an invalid, after 38 years of paralysis, it's against the rules for him to celebrate his new lease on life? What sort of religious people get their kicks out of enforcing rules like that? I guess they think this man was made for the rules.

The man knows he is in trouble. So what does he do? Well, he blames Jesus. Listen to him: "The man who healed me said to me, 'Pick it up and walk.'" And for the second time, we are disappointed in this man's response. Why does he finger Jesus? Wasn't it Jesus who made him well?

Our frustration with this man begins to grow. For when the rule keepers press him for the name of his healer, he has no idea who it is. He does not even know the identity of the one who made him well.

Later, Jesus finds him in the temple and says, "You look great! You are well again." Instead of thanking his healer, the man scurries off to the rule keepers. When he finds them, he tells them it was Jesus who compelled him to pick up his bedroll on the Sabbath. He rats on Jesus! He exposes Jesus to the very people who want to persecute him.

Frankly, our irritation with this man has reached a fever pitch. Why does Jesus bother with the guy? Why did he heal him in the first place? I mean, what's going on in this story?

Well, there's something pretty special going on here. But you really can't appreciate it, unless you go back one chapter in John's Gospel. Remember the story of the royal official from Capernaum whose son is dying (4:43-54)? This royal official learns that Jesus performs miracles. So in good faith, he travels 20 miles to Cana and begs Jesus to heal his son. He reasons that if Jesus can turn water into wine, he can heal his dying son. When Jesus says, "Your son lives," he takes him at his word and returns to Capernaum. When he arrives home, his servants greet him with the news that his son lives. Now he knows for sure that he can trust Jesus. You see, this story is all about faith; it's about the search of faith, a search motivated by the man's conviction that Jesus could help him in his hour of need.

But in our story, there is no mention of faith. The lame man gives no hint of faith in Jesus. He doesn't even know the name of his benefactor. And when the story ends, there is no indication that the man has come to faith. You see, our story is not about the man's faith; it's about God's grace. Jesus takes the initiative in this story. He heals the man. He grants him health. He takes the initiative not once, but twice. You see, Jesus is revealing something about God. That's what he does in every story of John's Gospel. Because of this story we know something about our God. Indeed, this story is a picture of God's grace in action.

So what does this story teach us about God's grace? We discover that his grace needs neither our doubt nor our faith. Do you remember the old bumper sticker "I found it"? It really doesn't say it very well, does it? For one does not find it, one gets found. The search of grace is not even frustrated by hostility or persecution. Jesus goes all the way to the cross. He reveals the truth that God himself is willing to suffer in order to give us life. He is our liberator; he is our Passover lamb.

If God's grace is strong enough to find this man at the pool, his grace is big enough to find us, and good enough to pursue us in spite of our dimwitted, irresponsible, and ungrateful reactions.

By the way, what were those puzzling words that Jesus spoke to the healed man: "Stop sinning or something worse may happen to you?" What's that supposed to mean? What could be worse than being an invalid for 38 years?

There's only one sin in John's Gospel and it's the sin of unbelief. It's the failure to believe that Jesus is the giver of eternal life—life that begins now and continues beyond the grave. In his final act of grace, Jesus implores the man to believe in him so that he might have life now and beyond the grave.

We don't know if this man ever embraced the grace that Jesus offered him. But we do know that the community for whom John wrote his Gospel embraced God's grace in Jesus Christ. Indeed, this community confesses in the Prologue: "And from his fullness we have all received grace upon grace" (1:16).

We too have received grace upon grace. And you know what? When you receive grace, you give grace to others. Like the bishop in the classic tale "Les Misérables," we may even turn our most treasured possessions over to people like Jean Valjean—vagrant convicts who cheat us, steal from us, and lie to us.

Grace means people don't get what they deserve. It means we treat each other better than we expect to be treated ourselves. Grace transcends justice. We meet a need expecting nothing in return. We forgive. We pay back insults with concern, even as the reformed Jean Valjean did when he took in a dying prostitute who had spat in his face, then went further by promising to care for her orphaned daughter, Cosette.

Trace an act of grace back to its roots, and you will find that ultimately its source is God. Follow an act of grace to its conclusion, and you will find that eventually it leads back to God.

The bishop received grace from God and passed it on to Jean Valjean. And when Valjean received the grace of God through the Bishop, he passed it on to a desperate women trapped in prostitution. And that's the way it is for us too, isn't it? Once we encounter God's grace in Jesus Christ, we pass it on to others. Grace begets grace.

Lowry's Method Evaluated

1. The Strength of Lowry's Method. The first notable strength of Lowry's narrative approach is its marriage of the form and content of biblical narrative texts with the form and content of the sermon. Since a major portion of the Bible is narrative, "narrative preaching is," as Holbert says, "...truer to the Bible's own narrative in its attention to form..." (1982: 25). Calvin Miller concurs: "The Bible is largely narrative; therefore, it follows that, if we are going to preach the Book, we need to remember that the Book is a 'story book'" (1992: 104). Hence, Lowry's method encourages the preacher to fit the form of the sermon to the form of the biblical text.

A second strength of Lowry's homiletical plot is his call to focus preaching on God's activity so that it, rather than human response or what we do, becomes the climax of the sermon. Surely this is an important emphasis if the gospel is to be heard with clarity today. His creation of a sermonic form that enables the listener to experience the gospel in terms of grace, freedom, and good news is clearly a commendable contribution. Lowry is persuaded that when the truth of the gospel intersects with the felt discrepancy of human experience, the Word happens and God speaks to us. Concerning the importance of focusing on God's activity in Christ, Elizabeth Achtemeier also emphasizes the activity of God. She aptly writes:

Many preachers spend most of their sermon time dwelling on human problems and never get around to saying what God is doing about them. It is easy to present the problems.... But it takes a preacher to tell what God is doing about the wrongs, and that activity of God should be the primary content of the sermon (1991: 49).

Thus, Lowry's plea to make the sermon a transforming event in time by focusing on God's activity in Christ at the climactic point of the sermon is to be applauded.

A third strength of Lowry's narrative model of preaching is its power to capture the attention of the people in today's pew. If, as Craddock suggests, the first goal of a sermon is to get heard, then Lowry's narrative plot sermonic form will be heard. Lowry defines plot as the moving suspense of story from disequilibrium to resolution. For Lowry, plot is the journey from "problematic itch" to "resolutional scratch." Lowry claims that, whether preaching a narrative text or not, in virtually all his sermons he moves from problem to solution, from itch to scratch. As Calvin Miller notes, "it is our hunger to have every itch scratched that makes the narrative sermon so all-consuming" (1992: 105). Thus, a commendable feature of Lowry's sermonic strategy is that in the unresolved tension his homiletical plot has the power to pull the listener along until the discrepancy is resolved.

A fourth strength of Lowry's narrative sermon strategy for preaching is its listener-oriented nature. Since Lowry encourages preachers to design sermons around an investigative search for a resolution to the text's problem or trouble, it overcomes many of the problems of the static outline and provides a way for the listeners to become active participants in the preaching moment. Craddock recognizes this listener-oriented value of narrative preaching when he says that "the shape of the communication is paramount in the business of effecting listener experience, and if the experience being sought is overhearing, the structure most congenial and with greatest potential for effectiveness is narrative" (1978: 135).

A fifth strength of Lowry's narrative approach relates to his attention to sermon preparation. Lowry has provided preachers with a veritable road map to sermon preparation and delivery. His three major works, *The Homiletical Plot, Doing Time In The Pulpit, and How To Preach A Parable,* are essentially handbooks on how to preach a narrative sermon. Richard L. Eslinger expresses his appreciation for this dimension of Lowry's work when he writes: "Little effort is needed to pry his methodological considerations loose from the more general homiletical discussion" (1987: 84-85).

A final strength of Lowry's narrative approach relates to his careful explanation of the paradigm shift required of those who wish to order experience rather than order ideas. Lowry has contrasted the radical differences between preaching based on ordering ideas versus preaching based on ordering experience. Anyone reading Lowry's discussion of the seven antitheses between ordering ideas and ordering experience cannot fail to grasp the difference between space-oriented discursive preaching and time-oriented narrative preaching. Richard L. Eslinger writes: "As well as anyone, Eugene Lowry has both portrayed the revolution in preaching and articulated the radical, systemic differences between ideational and narrative-based models" (1987: 85).

2. The Weakness of Lowry's Method. The first weakness of Lowry's narrative approach is that it may be a method that requires more creativity than the average preacher possesses. To be sure, Lowry recognizes that creativity is a factor in preparing narrative sermons and hence he anticipates this criticism by suggesting that creativity is not a gift possessed by the few but rather a potential result stimulated by choosing the right behavioral patterns. However, Ronald E. Seeth's cautionary remarks about narrative preaching are worth quoting here.

A final caution as to the use of story comes at the point

of aesthetics. The preacher who embraces narrative is often vitally interested in literature, theater, music, and other art expressions, which provide form and often content for storytelling.... However, many [cultural manifestations] assume a creative bent and training many preachers do not have. It could be possible that it is more difficult for a working pastor to master aesthetics than dogmatics or exegesis. The reservation is simply that the entire realm of narrative, parable, and story is opening up important creative areas for the preacher, but we ought to remember that such a realm will be affected by one's own background, training, and interest. In short, some will handle creativity more easily than others in this area, just as in other fields (1986: 98).

More than one writer warns that Lowry's method is not easy to master. Indeed, it is a method that requires reading and re-reading his suggested stages, making a point to know what each stage requires the preacher to do and how each step fits into the whole movement of the sermon.

A second weakness of Lowry's narrative approach relates to the purpose and scope of his narrative plot form. He maintains that he does not use the five step homiletical plot form when preaching biblical narrative for biblical narrative has its own plot form. Hence, he rejects the idea of superimposing his narrative plot form on biblical narrative. Instead, he suggests that the purpose of a narrative plot form is to make any sermon—life situational, doctrinal or expository—a narrative event. Thus, while Lowry refuses to impose his five step homiletical plot form on biblical narrative, he is quite willing to impose it on non-narrative biblical texts, thereby ignoring their peculiar literary forms. While it is entirely appropriate for the message of a biblical narrative to be captured by a narrative sermonic form, it is inconsistent for Lowry to superimpose his homiletical plot form on non-narrative biblical texts.

A third weakness in Lowry's narrative form concerns its purported ability to lead the listener to the same new insights the preacher experienced while preparing the ser-

mon. Lowry's homiletical plot strategy with its sudden reversal or loop attempts to lead the listeners to the place
where they suddenly say, "Aha! I have discovered a new
truth!" However, while the preacher may indeed gain new
insights during the process of preparing to preach, "it is
not at all clear," says Thomas Long, "that marching someone else through those steps will generate the same 'Eureka!'" (1989: 100).

A fourth weakness of Lowry's narrative plot is related
to its strength, namely, its problem-solving normative pattern. Lowry recently stated that back in 1970 he observed
that virtually all his sermons were "moving from problem
to solution, from itch to scratch...." Indeed, he claims this
simple problem-solution format became more detailed,
and his "homiletical plot" was born (Robinson 1990: 72).
Yet, Lowry's homiletical plot remains a problem-solving
sermonic form, although he labels it "narrative." While
the problem-solving form works to create listener interest
as noted above, the concern here is, as Thomas Long
states, that "the preacher will be tempted to form every
sermon to a pattern so well received" (1989: 100). Moreover, if the problem-solving strategy is repeatedly employed in the pulpit Sunday after Sunday, it may lead the
people to incorrectly conclude that the gospel's goal is
solving problems. The gospel is too rich and complex to
be proclaimed through a single sermonic form.

CHAPTER THREE

Buttrick's Motion-Picture Strategy

Rational homiletics, laments Buttrick, tends to reduce biblical texts to single propositional truths; it is a method that treats biblical passages as if they were still-life pictures full of details to be studied and talked about in a sermon. Instead, he invites preachers to think of biblical passages as "film-clips from motion pictures" (1981: 53). Biblical texts have movement and meaning occurs in movement as it travels from one understanding to another. Accordingly, he urges the contemporary preacher to favor mobile systems of sermon construction as opposed to fixed categorical development: "Sermon construction ought to travel through congregational consciousness as a series of immediate thoughts, sequentially designed and imaged with technical skill so as to assemble in forming faith" (1981: 55-56).

First, I will consider Buttrick's theology of preaching, which attempts to answer the question, why do preachers preach? Then, I will provide a sample sermon by David Buttrick and explain its components so that the reader can experience a sermon whose parts have been shaped like motion-picture film clips. Next, I will summarize his phenomenological approach to preaching by discussing his understanding of the various components and overall design of the sermon, including some of the detailed advice he gives for preparing a "moves" sermon. Finally, I will assess Buttrick's motion-picture homiletical approach, noting its strengths and weaknesses, and implement his approach, supplying a sermon that is based on the text of John 15.

Buttrick's Theology of Preaching

According to Buttrick, the biblical record speaks of two

kinds of preaching. There is out-church preaching to the unconverted by the laity in order to evangelize and there is in-church preaching to the faithful by the clergy in order to edify. The former leads to incorporation into a being-saved community in the world and the latter leads to the maturation of the being-saved community in the world (1987: 225-234).

Buttrick insists that preaching shapes the very character of the church. Preaching forms the spirit of the church and directs its purposes. He looks at the Reformers who set the voice of preaching up over the church and invites us to reclaim the Reformer's vision: "Preaching is God's Word to us" (1994: 42). He quotes Luther with approval: "The church comes into being because God's Word is spoken" (1987: 31). Unfortunately, laments Buttrick, we have lost sight of the Reformer's vision of the preached Word sustaining and reforming the life of the church. By mid-twentieth century a renewed ecclessiology reminded the church that it is a ministering community and a community of ministers. However, the emphasis on the good news of the liberation of the laity shifted the spotlight from pulpit to pew. In the shuffle, claims Buttrick, the notion that preaching is somehow the voice of God vanished (1994: 2).

He reminds us of the Reformers dictum: "God was *Deus loquens*, a speaking God." If we ask the Reformers, "how does God speak?", they answer: "Preaching is the Word of God" (1994: 21). The phrase, "Word of God," on the lips of the Reformers, refers to preaching the gospel message or *kerygma*. For the Reformers, preaching was Word of God and "scripture was also Word of God insofar as it proclaimed the same gospel message" (1994: 22-23).

In our century, we have run away from the Reformer's high theology of preaching. We seem to believe that "the whole notion of being the voice of God is, to say the least, somewhat intimidating" (1994: 29). But we need to recall that God has always chosen to speak through broken human agents, at least that is the testimony of scripture. Also, we need to reaffirm that preaching is the Word of God to us, "if, instigated by the Spirit, it serves God's redemptive purposes" (1994: 31).

One's definition of preaching and method of preaching are inextricably connected (1987: 297). Preaching is often defined either in relation to Christ and scripture, or in relation to experience and tradition. Buttrick rejects all definitions of preaching based on models of authority that maintain an objective and subjective split. Instead, he embraces a functional definition of preaching. Preaching is mediation. Preachers speak of God to people through Jesus Christ. "Preaching ... speaks of Mystery in the presence of Mystery; speaks from a consciousness of Consciousness that is conscious of us" (1987: 250). But more, preachers speak of God to people who are worldly human beings filled with fragments of understanding yet harboring huge mysteries. Preachers speak through Jesus Christ. Revelation, for Christians, is Jesus Christ who mediates God-for-humanity and humanity-for-God. Preachers do not simply address human beings in the world, they speak to Christian congregations that may be termed "being-saved communities" in the world. So then, what does preaching do? "Preaching calls" writes Buttrick, "to common mind the gospel of Jesus Christ, crucified and risen, as the gospel of liberation, our being-saved in the world" (1987: 255). What qualifies preachers to speak? Instead of pointing to such matters as vocational call, special insight, conversion experience, expert knowledge or spiritual compulsion, Buttrick invites us to begin by recognizing the representative humanity of those who preach. The person in the middle, who speaks as mediator, is simply a member of a being-saved community who preaches as a sinner among sinners (1987: 255-257).

Having defined preaching as mediation, Buttrick argues that preachers work with a double hermeneutic. They read texts from the past and study situations in the present. Since preaching is "through Jesus Christ," preachers study ancient texts like the New Testament and Hebrew scriptures in order to become acquainted with Christ Jesus. But they inevitably interpret Jesus Christ in the light of their awareness of being part of a being-saved community in the world. Preaching interprets being-saved in community in the world in the light of revelation. "In sum," writes

Buttrick, "the hermeneutical work of preaching is twofold: We interpret revelation in light of being-saved, and we grasp being-saved in view of revelation" (1987: 261).

Why do preachers preach? Buttrick finds no obvious social justification for preaching, but he does find reasons for preaching on the basis of theological reflection (1987: 449-459). Indeed, he embraces a rich theology of preaching consisting of the following five ideas.

1. Preaching is a continuation of the preaching of Jesus Christ. Scripture portrays Jesus Christ preaching, declaring the arrival of God's kingdom, and calling for faith and repentance. Immediately he called twelve disciples to follow him and in doing so he created a symbolic community of persons who would share his declarative ministry. Indeed, after his resurrection, which certified the truth of his message and gave the community salvific new life, Jesus commissioned the community, which understood itself to be a "being-saved" new humanity and witness to the resurrection, to continue his preaching in the world. Buttrick concludes: "So we are a joined-to-Jesus-Christ community, given life by resurrection, which continues the preaching of Jesus in the world" (1987: 451).

2. Christ continues to speak to the church and world through preaching. Language, or linguistic explosions, is generated by events, but language often dies. The durability of the language of the gospel generated by the Christ-event is astounding. Though modified over the centuries, the language of the gospel continues because Christian preaching interprets the reality of being-saved in the world, revealing the mystery of God-with-us. Convinced that words mediate reality as the Spirit speaks through Christ's broken yet risen community, Buttrick argues that Christian preaching continues the work of Christ as it calls, liberates and forms a new humanity. In this way, Buttrick posits a christological, rather than an institutional motive, for preaching. "We do not preach so the church may survive, or gain members, or triumph in the world," writes Buttrick. Rather, "we preach so Christ may use our words in a salvific work, revealing and redeeming" (1987: 252).

3. The aim of preaching is the reconciliation of the

world. When Scripture speaks of being "saved" as it does in John 3:16, it envisions a new social reality that is counter to the notions of personal salvation, human potential, and social progress. Salvation, biblically understood, is reconciliation that sets people free for the love of God and neighbors. Thus, preaching, which Buttrick believes shares in God's saving purposes, is a liberating word that sets people free from both psychological and social forms of bondage. Also, true preaching, although an interim activity based on a past event and operative until Christ's return, participates in God's dynamic present activity in our midst.

4. *Preaching evokes response*. The response to preaching is a response to Christ, and is, properly, faith and repentance. Buttrick corrects several misconceptions about the relationship between faith and repentance, noting that faith and repentance are not sequential responses but facets of the same reality that interface. Also, he notes that faith and repentance are motions of the soul that are related to the new social reality Jesus inaugurated, not simply motions of the soul related to the person of Christ. He insists: "We believe not merely in Jesus, but in Jesus Christ as inaugurator of the kingdom" (1987: 454). The response of faith and repentance is made possible by the preaching of the gospel. He qualifies his remarks by rejecting any notion that the way the gospel is preached will determine positive response, or conversely, that if preached rightly the gospel will somehow be free of negative response. To be sure, preachers should shun arrogance, obtuseness, assertiveness, and self-righteousness in the pulpit. Rejection of the preached gospel comes with the turf of preaching. "If we do preach good news of a new order in Christ Jesus it will be received gladly by some (usually those who are broken) but may be rejected by others (usually those who are 'together' and have 'made it big')" (1987: 455). Moreover, since the gospel calls us to live in God's new social order, a believing response will necessitate alterations in our self-understanding. Even our "decisions" are a result of the formative power of God's grace preached. Buttrick explains: "We heard the gospel preached and it changed our minds. We were in the presence of a being-saved community which, to some extent, displayed the new age" (1987: 456). Finally, Buttrick warns that preachers should not anticipate either widespread approval or praise of their preaching. Preaching is a no-win situation. "We can never greet opposition as sure evidence of sin...and we can never bask in praise as if we are any more than mediators, the servants of grace" (1987: 456).

5. *Preaching is the Word of God.* He does not link preaching with the "Word of God" without qualification. The bald statement—preaching is the "Word of God"— does not mean that the preacher's voice is to be equated with the voice of God. He says, "though we preach knee deep in grace, we can claim no status for our words" (1987: 456). Conversely, preachers should not reduce their sermons to human works of art or eloquence and lose sight of its mystery. Preaching is a peculiar vocation in so far as God claims, converts, and saves through our words simply because we continue what Christ began. "Christ transfers preaching to us, and gives grace to our speaking, so that, as odd as it may seem, our sermons are Word of God to human communities" (1987: 457). Still, we must also avoid a spiritualist understanding of preaching that bypasses our humanity. Neither struggle nor spontaneity in the pulpit is evidence of the Spirit's presence or absence. Following Luther's lead, Buttrick says: "The presence of the Spirit is not self-evident but is, indeed, an article of faith—of homiletic faith" (1987: 457). Ultimately, the acid test of the Spirit's presence is neither our struggles, nor our spontaneities, but rather the edification of the faith community. While insisting that preaching is the "Word of God," he distances himself from fundamentalist positions that make careful repetition or interpretation of Scripture the guarantee that preaching is the Word of God. Instead, he claims that "God is free even from our fidelities! So, let us be willing to say baldly that it is possible to preach the Word of God without so much as mentioning scripture" (1987: 458). While we delight in, live with, and study scripture, preaching scripture does not guarantee that a sermon will

be the Word of God. While a preacher's character may prompt the public to ridicule the gospel, what we say cannot be devalued by who we are. For the gospel's efficacy and content are not determined by our character. "We ourselves are never Word of God" (1987: 458).

In the final analysis, says Buttrick, what's critical for preachers is confidence in the gospel, trust in God's grace, and prayer for the Spirit's presence. Although our words are human, if they "are instigated by Jesus Christ, serve God's salvific purpose, and are ratified by the Spirit with a being-saved-community, they are Word of God" (1987: 459).

Sample Sermon by Buttrick

"The Sacrifice of Abraham" is a sermon by David Buttrick and is reproduced here to illustrate both his theology of preaching and his motion-picture strategy (1987: 357-360). It is based on the texts of Genesis 22:1-19 and Revelation 5:11-14. Please read the biblical texts prior to reading the sermon.

Sermon
"The Sacrifice of Abraham"

An old German woodcut pictures the sacrifice of Isaac. There is Isaac, all trussed up, lying on a pile of brush; huge empty-circle eyes, staring. Above him stands Abraham, both hands held high, about to plunge the knife. Over to one side, in a bush, stands a white lamb, waiting. What a strange story! The story has troubled religious people for centuries, everyone from Augustine to Kafka, from Kierkegaard to Karl Barth. What can we make of the sacrifice of Isaac? Terror and grace. What can we make of the story?

At the outset, notice: Isaac is much more than an only child. Isaac is hope, hope wrapped up in human flesh. All the promises of God were riding on Isaac. Remember the story? Remember how God dropped in to tell Sarah and Abraham that their offspring would be as many as the sands of the sea that they would give birth to nations? Well, the old folks giggled, for, according to reliable medical advice, it's mighty tough to conceive when you're pushing ninety! Then, suddenly, Isaac was born, a miracle child: God did provide! Through Isaac, there would be many descendants, a multitude of nations. An American playwright tells of how his Jewish parents scrimped and saved to give him everything. They bought him new clothes three times a year, bundled him off to private schools, paid for his college education. "Everything we got is wrapped up in you, boy!" his mother used to say. "Everything we got is wrapped up in you." How easy it is to focus our hopes. God gives us a land to live in and, before you know it, we're chanting, "Everything we've got is wrapped up in you, America!" Or a church to belong to: "Everything we've got is wrapped up in you, Presbyterian Church!" Listen, Isaac was more than an only child. Isaac embodied the promises of God. "Everything we got is wrapped up in you, boy." Isaac was hope, all the hope in the world.

So what happened? God spoke. "Kill him off," said God, "Take your only child and kill him!" We hear the words and we're appalled. We've always talked of God as Love, spelled L-O-O-O-V-E, so hard words shake us. "Kill him off," said God. Suddenly life is not what we thought it was—comfortable therapist's office on a couch called "prayer" we can spill out our souls to some caring Deity. No, instead, we're stuck with a stony place, a funeral pyre, and a knife blade flashing. Yes, God gives good gifts, but God takes away! "All our loves," cries the heroine of a British novel, "All our loves, you take away!" For every brimming child, there does seem to be a knife blade. So maybe, as the theologians say, we're going to have to "reconstruct our God-concept" to include a few of the darker shades. God may well be terribly good, but notice the adverb "terribly"! God spoke a terrible word to Abraham. As Abraham stood staring at his child Isaac, God said, "Kill him. Kill him off." God spoke.

Then, of all things, Abraham obeyed. Abraham did as he was told. He obeyed. Flat-eyed, grim, Abraham led his son up the hill, muttering "God will provide," "God will provide," with biting irony. Fanatic Abraham obeyed. To most of us, religion's rather easygoing, a "liberal persuasion," something that's even passable on campus—you can talk religion down at The University Club. Then, we flip a page in our Bible and stumble on wild-eyed Abraham passing out the poisoned Kool-Aid in some stony Jonestown, and we're embarrassed. Down in the Southwest there's a tribe, the Penitentes. Some say they were practicing human sacrifice into the 1950s. Finally, they were investigated. "What kind of people are you to practice human sacrifice?" a prosecutor demanded. To which a tribal leader replied, "You do not take God seriously." Well, maybe we don't. We are moderate people: We calculate our charities, confess our minimal sins, schedule a "Minute for Mission" on a weekly basis, and run for dear life from anything in excess. But, see, in Abraham, radical, blind obedience. God commanded, and Abraham was bent on doing God's will even if it meant slaughtering his only hope. So, Abraham went up the hill to kill Isaac. God spoke and Abraham obeyed.

Now, hear the clatter of the knife on stone. See Abraham's arms fold down to his side. For, suddenly, Abraham caught sight of the trapped lamb: "God will provide," he cried triumphantly. "God will provide!" Well, if you're Christian, you can't help thinking of Calvary, can you? Of another stone hill, and a high cross. One of the earliest pictures of the crucifixion is a Byzantine wall painting. The picture shows the stone hill and the wood-stick cross, but, instead of hung Jesus, there's a huge nailed lamb on the crossbar: Lamb of God! Look, if God will hand over an only Child as sacrifice to our rigid sins, then see, behind the hard hurt surface of life, there's not a Holy Terror, but Love: Love so amazing, so Divine, so unutterly intense it will sacrifice itself for us. Lamb on the cross, then Lamb on the Throne! So, Abraham caught sight of the trapped lamb and shouted for joy. Clatter of the knife on stone. Fold of the arm, "God will provide," cried Abraham.

Now, do you see what the sacrifice of Abraham is all about? God set Abraham free for faith. The Bible calls the story a "test" but the word is too tame. On a high stone hill, God set Abraham free, free for faith. Blind obedience was transformed into faith. Oh, how easy it is to pin all our hopes on a means of grace, and forget God, the giver. Subtly we turn God's gifts into idols. God has given us the scriptures, but see how we flank the open page with candles and frame dogma to guarantee infallibility: "Everything we've got is wrapped up in you, Bible." Or, perhaps, God draws us into faith through a masculine church; before you know it we're protecting the pronouns and two-legged tailored vestments: "Everything we got's wrapped up in you," sung by a bass-voiced choir. Back in the sixties, a liberal Catholic journal announced gleefully, "God can get along without the Latin Mass." To which a reader replied: "Maybe God can, but we can't." Is there any idolatry like religious idolatry? No wonder God speaks and shatters our souls: "Kill it off?" God who takes away all our false loves. So, on a high hill, God called up Abraham and Isaac, and there—Amazing, Ruthless Grace—God set Abraham free, free for faith.

Well, here we are stumbling down a stone-hill Calvary into the twentieth century. We are free to trust God, for God will provide. Oh, we still have our Bible, our church, our liturgies, but, somehow, they are different now: the gilded sheen has rubbed off. We can love our churches, without having to hold on for dear life, particularly in an age when God may be sweeping away our denominations. And, yes, we can love the scriptures, without having to defend each sacred page, especially now when authority fights are building. We can trust the self-giving God to give us all we'll ever need: "God will provide!" There's a minister in a northern state who has papered a wall of her office: Custom-made wallpaper repeating words line after line, all over the space. Now she can sit at her desk and read: "Trust God, Let go. Trust God, Let go." Because we trust God—Lamb on the throne—we can let go of all our loves: Bible, church, nation, even sexuality. We can stumble down from Calvary into a human world, sure of the grace of God.

Now then, here are pictures to put up in your mind. A stone hill, a pile of brush, empty-circle eyes, a knife blade high. "Kill him off," cracks the voice of God. But, here's another picture: A wood cross on a rock hill, and a lamb nailed to the crossbar, "God will provide." Keep both pictures in your mind. "You God, you take away all our loves, but you give yourself!" Trust God, let go. Let go, trust God.

Analysis of Buttrick's Sermon

At this stage in our study of Buttrick's approach to preaching, it may be helpful to "exegete" the sample sermon entitled "The Sacrifice of Abraham."

First, Buttrick prefers to speak of narrative sermons as "preaching in the mode of immediacy" (1987: 362). This sermon has six "moves," a term he uses to refer to the smaller units of the sermon. He also uses the term "moves" to underscore the movement of language as opposed to static points. The sermon is framed by both an introduction and conclusion. The introduction, which con-

sists of nine short, crisp sentences, sets the stage for the
first move and identifies the characters of the biblical story. It also places the story in its religious context. The description of the German woodcut picture of the Genesis
story puts the focus on an image rather than on questions
of historicity. The introductory question ("What can we
make of the story?") functions nicely to conclude the introduction and prepare the listener for the first move of the
sermon. The conclusion of the sermon is also brief—eight
concise sentences! It invites the listeners to keep both pictures in mind. That is, both the Old Testament picture of
Abraham's sacrifice and the New Testament picture of
God's sacrifice. Notice that the conclusion also picks up
various images from the sermon, especially phrases from
moves three, four and six. Buttrick is striving to shape the
faith consciousness of the community.

Second, each move consists of a theological idea drawn
from the biblical text, in this case, the texts of Genesis 22
and Revelation 5. In addition, each move consists of analogies of experience that are developed in anticipation of congregational blocks. The first move places the biblical story
against the theological backdrop of God's covenant promises to Abraham. It does this by means of an act of memory. "Remember how God dropped in to tell Sarah and
Abraham...." The background information is then illustrated with a contemporary Jewish story with its crucial sentence: "Everything we got is wrapped up in you, boy!" This
key sentence of the contemporary story is then connected
to the listeners and their own tendency as God's people to
treat country and denomination in the same way. Finally,
note how the first move, like the subsequent moves, begins
and ends with two or three simple sentences that emphasize the single idea of the move. In this way, Buttrick hopes
his listeners will hear the idea of the move.

Third, with the second move, the action of the biblical
story begins. But notice that there is little actual description of the story itself. Instead, Buttrick uses contemporary
language that imitates God's command to Abraham and
spells out our reaction to its harsh reality. In this way, he
avoids turning to the past and then to the present in the

sermon. The move develops and focuses our reaction to God's shocking command to Abraham. Again, notice the size of the move, specifically the economy of words. It may take the preacher only 3 1/2 minutes to communicate the entire second move. The third move treats Abraham's obedience and also focuses on the next logical event in the biblical story. The narrative begins with God's command and resumes with Abraham's obedience.

Fourth, in the next move, Buttrick imitates the suspense of the biblical story. Abraham catches sight of the lamb in the thicket. Buttrick introduces the Christian consciousness of Calvary but within the Genesis story. Thus, we are introduced to the Christian message of God's love without explicit mention of Christ dying as a sacrifical lamb—an idea foreign to the Genesis story. In the fifth move, Buttrick interprets the Genesis idea of "test" in terms of the notion of freedom. Abraham was set free to trust the giver himself, rather than simply the giver's gifts.

Fifth, in the final move, Abraham's movement down from Mount Moriah is analogous to the Christian's movement down from Calvary. It explores Abraham's radical trust in God and the Christian's trust in God granted by means of the cross of Christ, setting us free to trust God rather than his gifts. Thus, Buttrick's sermon illustrates his desire to attend to the smaller units of a sermon as well as its overall shape and motion. He wants us as preachers to think in terms of shaping the consciousness of our hearers.

Buttrick's Phenomenological Approach

Since the Protestant Scholastics of the eighteenth century, a rationalistic approach to preaching has dominated the homiletical horizon. Sermons have been designed largely by following a rigid scheme that included "careful understanding, explication and application," notes Buttrick (1981: 46). Over the years, this aged pattern was slightly modified as preachers attempted to reduce passages to a single theme stated in a proposition. As a result a stock homiletic design emerged that is with us to this day: "An introduction was followed by the text, which was in turn reduced to a propositional topic, which was developed in a series of 'points' (often categorical), before the sermon ended in a conclusion" (1981: 47). Later, this rational homiletic was altered. The preacher, on the basis of prayer and subjective pastoral interactions with the congregation, would discover a sermonic idea, locate a text that embodied the idea, and then preach the sermon in a series of "points." "The result," writes Buttrick, "is that now we have a romantic concept of 'inspiration' coupled with a rational method, a mix found in most homiletic texts today" (1987: 47). Still later, Harry Emerson Fosdick approached sermons by beginning with the personal problems of the people, summarizing religious truths that addressed their problems, and concluding with an illustration. In Buttrick's judgment, Fosdick's personalistic approach "violated the corporate ethic of the New Testament and led directly to the 'triumph of the therapeutic' in recent American preaching" (1981: 48).

Buttrick is troubled by rational homiletics. First, as a method of preaching, it is no accident that it emerged at the same time as the scientific method, which operates by isolating an object for study and making descriptive statements based on a general deduction. He doubts that "a rational, objective method can cope with biblical language which is often figural, poetic, or narrative in form" (1981: 47). Second, rational homiletics, which developed at about the same time that eighteenth century rationalism was attacking biblical narrative, presupposes that single texts contain propositional truths or principles for preaching. "By distilling 'truths' acceptable to general religious experience," says Buttrick, "the church could maintain a semblance of intellectual respectability in a difficult era" (1981: 47). Third, rational homiletics treated biblical passages as if they were still life picture in which something may be located. What was ignored is the "composition of the 'picture,' the narrative structure, the movement of the story" (1981: 49). Fourth, the distillation method of rational homiletics produced point-making sermons that were exercises in rational observation. Unfortunately, what's wrong with point-making sermons is that they are not only intrinsically tedious, but they are simultaneously static and didactic. "Categorical systems are easy, but only for clergy," notes Buttrick. "Because they are static and have no moving excitement—What will happen next?—they are hard to listen to in a congregation" (1994: 84).

The rationalist, scientific worldview is disappearing, argues Buttrick, for it failed to recognize that reality is beyond both objective and subjective categories. "Reality," writes Buttrick, "is defined by consciousness" (1994: 79). What is needed today are new ways of preaching for an emerging new human consciousness. Indeed, homiletic method, insists Buttrick, "is much more than a how-to-program for desperate preachers; it is a strategy for the presentation of the gospel in a strange, turbulent new age" (1994: 80).

Buttrick reluctantly acknowledges that his proposed homiletic strategy may be described as "phenomenological" (1987: xii). It is a term that points to his interest in understanding what actually happens in human consciousness when preparing and hearing a sermon. Also, it accents his conviction that biblical language is intentional, performative, and designed to function in consciousness. The sermon attempts to do rhetorically what the text does rhetorically. The sermon is less concerned with the meaning of the text and more concerned with how the language of the text functions. During sermon preparation, instead of searching for the meaning of the content of the text, the preacher tries to discover what the text wants to do and takes from the scriptural text a rhetorical strategy for preaching. While the sermon embodies the meaning of the content of the text, this homiletician is more concerned with the sermon's function: "preaching shapes the faith-consciousness of the church" (1987: 17, 20, and 41).

The modern decline in the market value of words prompts Buttrick to develop a "slapdash phenomenology of language" in an effort to restore appreciation for words. There are two kinds of language: naming and story. Naming constitutes our world and story confers identity in the world. Buttrick's natural theology of language has serious implications for preaching because, he says, story and naming are the stuff of preaching. "Preaching," writes Buttrick, "can rename the world 'God's world' with metaphorical power, and can change identity by incorporating all our stories into 'God's story.' Preaching can construct in consciousness a 'faith-world' related to God" (1987: 11).

By definition, writes Buttrick,

> Christian preaching tells a story and names a name. If narrative consciousness confers identity, then preaching transforms identity, converts in the truest sense of the world, by rewriting our stories into a God-with-us story—beginning, Presence, and end. In view of the great disclosure of Gratuitous Love, by metaphor, preaching renames the human world as a space for new humanity related to God. What preaching may do is to build in consciousness a new 'faith-world' in which we may live and love! (1987: 16-17).

With these words Buttrick accents preaching's functional role in building a faith-world in human consciousness. Preaching is not defined as conversion, or as imparting revealed truths, or as solving life's problems, or as providing inspirational uplifts. It is best defined as forming faith consciousness.

I will now explore six aspects of Buttrick's approach, including hermeneutics, homiletics, moves, framework, language, and image. It is important to remember that some of these terms are peculiar to Buttrick's homiletical method.

1. Preaching as Hermeneutics. Here we will explore Buttrick's discussion of the shape of hermeneutics for preaching, paying special attention to his understanding of the history, meaning, and intention of biblical texts. He poses two critical hermeneutical questions: (1) How do texts, clearly products of an earlier age and reflecting an ancient worldview, articulate today? (2) How can words written in an earlier age to a different people have anything to say to us today in a twenty-first century time and place? How can words bridge time?

He makes three hermeneutical proposals (1987: 264-279). First, the recipients of biblical texts are faith communities. Indeed, even when addressed to individuals, the persons in question share a communal Christian consciousness. Thus, when interpreting the text, the exegete must determine what it says to "our communal faith consciousness." Second, Buttrick insists that biblical texts address our bi-focal communal consciousness of being in the world and being-saved in the world. All biblical texts will address our communal consciousness of being shaped by the human world in which we live as well as our consciousness of being-saved in the world. Third, the Bible must be interpreted within an interaction of symbol and story for it exhibits both a narrative consciousness and symbolic consciousness. "Why does the Bible tell stories and brood over symbols," asks Buttrick. "Precisely because the Bible is speaking of God's Presence-in-Absence amid mysteries of being in the world" (1987: 279).

There is always the possibility of misinterpretation, acknowledges Buttrick. After all, we all approach the study of texts with all kinds of methodological, theological, and cultural baggage. However, we can do three things to guard against misinterpretation (1987: 280). First, it is not inappropriate to view our interpretations with a measure of distrust for we are perspectival. We read the text through a multitude of convictional lenses. Second, interpretation is assisted by our double consciousness of being-saved in the world. Such a consciousness enables us to differentiate the "mind" of being-saved from the "mind" of our world-age. Third, we need to exploit all kinds of critical methods for approaching the text, not limiting our methodological options, nor failing to develop new methodological skills. Fourth, since preachers speak their interpretations to a being-saved community, he proposes three tests of interpretation:

(1) Does interpretation align the mysteries of being-in-the-world with the Mystery disclosed through symbols of revelation? (2) Does interpretation serve to define being-saved in relation to being-in-the-world and vice versa? (3) Does interpretation invoke the Presence in Mystery

through Jesus Christ, story and symbol? In short, does interpretation lead to mediation? (1987: 281).

2. Preaching and Homiletics. While the older homiletic approaches spoke of outlines and purpose, Buttrick speaks of plot and intention. "Preaching involves the designing of 'plots' for consciousness and a wielding of 'intentional' language" (1987: 285). It is especially important to understand Buttrick's use of the term plot and the term intention.

Sermons are plotted scenarios that aim to form a congregation's faith-consciousness. Note three things about plot. First, he makes a distinction between history and plot. Scripture does not contain history, but rather a series of calculated plots. By the term history he means "an event in its fullness—what actually takes place" (1987: 285). However, to relate to others the fullness of any event experienced in time requires entering so many fields of consciousness and so many perspectives that what we tend to do in telling others about an event is select and order. Indeed, what we tend do is relate events to others in representative fashion by constructing plots. "Plot is never arbitrary," says Buttrick, "but is formed in consciousness by an interaction of audience and the hermeneutic of a teller" (1987: 286).

Second, the history of any event comprises a cluster of characters and series of episodes. Even if a storyteller is capable of absorbing a whole event in his field of consciousness, in retelling the event the storyteller breaks into a sequence, re-plotting the material. There are several components of plotting. One factor is the hermeneutical consciousness of the storytellers whose plots are structured under the influence of his convictions about life, philosophy, theology, and morals. Another component includes the type of genre selected for telling the story and the choice of conventional repertoires. Yet another component of plotting is point-of-view. In each plot, attitudinal or temporal shifts in distance may occur. Still another component of plotting is the logic of movement for plots travel along episode by episode. Finally, in the process of telling a story the teller selects a strategy for shaping the plot so that it functions in audience consciousness.

Third, preaching is a form of plotting for it inevitably involves structuring. Sermons emerge from a preacher's consciousness which has been shaped by the interpretation of a text into a whole field of theological meaning. Since the preacher desires to form faith consciousness in his audience, the sermon will involve the designing of plots, or moves, that betray a logic of movement dictated by a theology (1987: 286-293).

The word intention is also important in Buttrick's homiletic. There will be no understanding of preaching until one grasps the idea of "intentionality." His ideas about intentionality are based on a simple analogy: human consciousness functions like a camera lens. The human mind focuses on a field of consciousness by backing up, widening out, drawing near, or narrowing down. Like a camera, we can employ filters and highlight certain structures of meaning. In consciousness we select our angles of vision for we perceive life like a camera. He applies this analogy between the human mind and a camera to the subject of preaching, making three points. First, there is an "intending of" when we preach. Our sermons focus on a field of understanding discerned in a biblical text, but within a given field they will bring into view, a specific structure of meaning. "In preaching a sermon on a passage, we will be projecting a field in congregational consciousness and intending a structure of understanding—perhaps, the mystery of God-with-us" (1987: 295).

Second, there is an "intending toward" when we preach. Preaching is always language aimed at communal consciousness, not individual consciousness. What preachers have in mind when preaching is an "inchoate gestalt of congregational consciousness" (1987: 296).

Third, there is an "intending to do" when we preach. The structure of meaning in consciousness which the preacher is trying to bring out and the preacher's "gestalt" of the congregation being addressed will dictate the sermon's purpose and strategy. He argues that the purpose of a sermon, its intending to do, is "a line of strategy drawn between an intending of and an intending toward" (1987:

298). Sermons are shaped then by what is being brought out of a field of consciousness and by structures of meaning within congregational consciousness.

Having explored the two terms of plot and intention, it is now possible to put them together. Proclamation is an intentional act. Sermons are a sequence of plotted moves put together in a scenario by some kind of strategy. Essentially, plots are determined by intention; plots are strategy. "All preaching is performative, an intending to do" (1987: 301). When preachers preach from scripture, they are engaged in replotting plots and reintending intentions for a new world in consciousness.

Buttrick rejects the frequent suggestion that there is a direct progression from text to sermon (Best 1978: 54-113). Instead, he argues that preachers move from (1) exegetical study to a (2) field of understanding, and then to the (3) production of a sermon. While the details of exegetical study need no comment here, the notion of a field of understanding requires elaboration. Once the exegetical work of study is complete, the first step in sermon preparation is the hermeneutical task of understanding that begins with plot analysis. The text is analyzed as plot by doing a semi-structural analysis of the passage verse by verse. Then, after outlining the plot, it is helpful to read the plot from a literary standpoint to see its design. Next, since the passage is a pattern of plot and intention, it is imperative to delineate the theological field of meaning underlying the passage. Finally, while engaged in the above exercises, the preacher is almost unconsciously drawing analogies between the text and his own world of experience. "Exegetical study of the text," says Buttrick, "as well as plot analysis, the delineation of a theological field, the drawing of analogies, all together produce in our consciousness a whole field of understanding" (1987: 308). For example, in a text like Matthew 2:1-12, the preacher discovers an underlying theological field of meaning: the coming of Christ is promise to some (Wisemen) and terrible threat to others (Herod).

A second major step in sermon preparation moves beyond the discovery of a theological field of meaning to breaking the whole meaning into a scenario of moves for speaking. Preaching involves replotting the biblical text. Such replotting is a process that goes through three stages: 1) forming a basic structure; 2) developing the structure; and 3) putting the developed structure into a script for preaching. It is important here to consider each of the three stages.

The first stage is forming a basic structure. Since scripture passages have different theological fields of meaning underlying them, they will require different basic sermonic designs. "There are no stock patterns into which meaning can invariably be stuffed," says Buttrick (1987: 308-309). Stock sermonic designs inevitably distort fields of understanding. Given the reality that all speaking involves movement, how does a preacher take a whole new field of meaning and break it into a sequenced scenario for preaching?

There are three factors involved in designing a basic structure. The initial factor is the point of entry into the field of understanding. This is an invitation to identify the starting point for filming the field of understanding that has formed in the preacher's consciousness. For example, in the text of Matthew 2:1-12, the preacher might begin with our world's contemporary longing for a new order of things which is really analogous to the Wisemen's question, where is he? When determining the point of entry into the field of understanding that has formed in the preacher's consciousness, the preacher must look at both the plot of the original passage and the analogies with our own world of experience.

The next factor is the logic of movement or the flow of subsequent ideas. Sometimes elements in the story or passage dictate the logic of movement. In Matthew 2:1-12, one could begin with Herod's reaction to the arrival of Christ, but then we would have to turn back to the reaction of the Wisemen in order to introduce the irony that for some Christ is savior and for others threat. "What we do in forming a basic structure," says Buttrick, "is to keep referring to the field of understanding where there are elements of meaning still available" (1987: 310).

A third factor relates to the way we think. The sequence of a sermon will not only be influenced by the shape of the biblical material but also by the way human consciousness functions. There is a rudimentary test for assessing a basic structure. Read the basic structure out loud in sequence to determine if it makes sense, asking if each phrase follows naturally. In short, in the first stage the preacher is designing the basic structure of a sermon that will mediate a field of understanding to congregational consciousness.

The second stage is developing or expanding the structure. A basic structure is clearly not a sermon. It consists of a few short sentences on a page. This second stage is more like a sermon "sketch" for it consists of winding ideas around a basic sentence structure and creating the rough shape of a sermon. "The trick in developing a sermon sketch," says Buttrick, "is to expand each single sentence in order by putting together theological understanding and lived experience" (1987: 313). What is intended here is not a finished sermon. There are several advantages to doing a sketch: first, it gets our thinking out into the open where we can critique it; second, it gives us some slight development of thought so that one can begin to think about images and illustrations; and third, it gets us started on the problems of internal design in each move (1987: 313-316).

The third stage is putting the developed structure into a script for preaching. Having criticized, imaged, and noted various developmental shapes, the preacher draws things together into a final structure. The final structure is more than a sketch but less than a sermon manuscript. In the process of moving from a field of understanding in consciousness to bare structure and then sketch, the sermon structure takes on its own detached life and becomes something that the preacher works on. As the preacher crafts the sermon structure into a final structure two processes are involved: first, the preacher works on the individual parts of each move clarifying language, internal design, and points-of-view; and second, the preacher will be working over the whole structure to ensure that moves interrelate, that logic of movement is clear and that style changes expressively (1987: 316).

Sermons can be designed in three different modes: the mode of immediacy, reflection, or praxis. A sermon in the *mode of immediacy* follows the preacher's immediate participation in the world of the biblical text, especially narratives. But the preacher does not simply retell the biblical story. He helps the congregation by relating the biblical and contemporary worlds. In a sermon in the *reflective mode* the plot follows the movement of the preacher's reflections. The moves of the sermon are moments of reflection on a passage. Paul's letters are especially suited to this mode. A sermon in the *mode of praxis* focuses on a topic. The plot of the sermon helps the congregation come to a better understanding of the situation.

3. Preaching In Moves. Buttrick speaks of sermons as bundles of words or talks ordered in sequences called "moves." He wants to avoid the older terminology of "points" for the word point implies a rational, at-a-distance pointing at things, some kind of objectification (1987: 23). He prefers to speak of sermons in terms of developing scenarios, or movements of thought tied together from beginning to end by some sort of logic.

He speaks from a background well informed by rhetoric, the study of words in motion. Instead of disparaging rhetoric, he demonstrates the necessity of an understanding of rhetoric for preaching. He observes that the movement of ideas in preaching is slower than everyday conversation and the attention span of today's congregation is short. So a preacher should take about four minutes for each conceptual idea of his sermon and twenty minutes for the entire sermon that has five or six sequenced subjects. A preacher strives to form conceptual understanding in communal consciousness by preaching a sermon that involves a sequence of subject matters arranged in some sort of structural design with each simple meaning developed into a move or a language module that is between three and four minutes in length (1987: 25).

Every move has an internal design determined by theological understanding, an eye for oppositions, and the actualities of lived experience. These three aspects of design influence how the preacher thinks-out an individual move for sermon presentation. Theological precision is critical because how we understand biblical ideas determines the images and the word-pictures we use in depicting the ideas to the congregation in each sermonic move. "Homiletic thinking is always a thinking of theology toward images," maintains Buttrick (1987: 29). Also, each move will be designed with a view to spotting opposition or resistance to the sermon and dealing with them. In particular, the preacher will shape the move with an eye on resistances to the gospel born of human sinfulness, cultural presuppositions, contemporary social attitudes, and religious distortions. Finally, each move will be shaped with an eye for the actualities of lived experience both in the social world as well as the world of the self-conscious (1987: 29-33).

As the preacher crafts each move with these three factors interacting with each other and shaping the move, a strategy for presenting the move emerges. "Moves must have clear, defined internal shape," says Buttrick, "else they will not form in congregational consciousness" (1987: 34). What's needed is more than a haphazardly collected cluster of thoughts but rather a carefully designed presentation that is governed by the content of the gospel of free grace and contemporary thought structures. Each move presents a single idea by means of a number of subordinate parts that have been shaped by some focused theological concept, careful consideration of congregational oppositions that might block understanding, and lived experiences. Preaching, a sophisticated form of public address, forms the faith-consciousness of the church on behalf of Jesus Christ.

Every move is built according to a specific blueprint. All moves have three parts: an opening statement, a closing statement and development in between. The opening statement of a move is usually preceded by a pause in speaking for audiences are most alert after a brief pause in a sermon. The beginning of the move is critical. The preacher must capture the listeners' attention in a few short sentences. While oblique starters may create suspense, the preacher should avoid the delayed start for they fail to focus consciousness and often irritate an audience.

Also, while a single key sentence will work in one-to-one conversation, it is inadequate in shaping group consciousness. What is required is a cluster of three reiterative sentences functioning as if they were one and focusing the subject of the move. The all-important goal of the opening statement is to fix the congregation's focus on the subject at hand like a camera lens zooming in on its target. The opening statement is difficult to prepare because of its multiple functions. In addition to fixing focus, the opening statement of a move must establish connective logic with the preceding move, the perspective of the move, and the mood of the move. "Unless each move, at the outset, structures in consciousness, a sermon will not mean!" (1987: 40).

The second part of an individual move is developing the focus idea. Since congregations consist of people who are being-saved in the world, they have a peculiar double consciousness. Drawing on rhetorical wisdom, he suggests that each move will develop from three basic rhetorical postures: first, preaching will involve bringing out various understandings of the Christian faith by means of explanation, metaphor, analysis, exploration, and analogy; second, preaching will include associating Christian convictions with lived experience by means of testimony, example, illustration, and imagery; and third, Christian preaching will disassociate or distinguish Christian understandings from other social attitudes and ideas. Of course, within each of these three rhetorical strategies, there may be different orientations labeled temporal, spatial, social, and personal (1987: 40-43).

The third part of a move is closure. If a single subject matter is to form in group consciousness, the preacher must return to the initial idea of the move and reiterate its focus at the conclusion of the move. The closing statement must always return to the starting idea of the move. What is required is not compound sentences, or questions, or quotations, but rather a simple, terse, final statement with a strong definite noun. Each move is developed differently and with care so that it will begin and end with sufficient strength to form faith in communal consciousness.

Every move then will have an opening statement, development, and then closure (1987: 108).

In practice, how does one develop a move? Ideas of development will come as the preacher thinks through theological meanings, cultural oppositions, lived experience, and rhetorical strategies. Several practical suggestions should be noted. First, while moves may contain single or two-part systems, they must not exceed three internal parts. For example, since we live between the ages, a contrapuntal system may be necessary in developing an idea. Contrapuntals, which "let off steam" within the move and recognize rather than reinforce oppositions, must not undermine or overpower the move statement. A second important factor in developing a move is variety. Each move should be shaped differently because similarity in developmental systems breeds boredom. Thus, "the general rule will be different development for different ideas" (1987: 48). A third factor in developing a move is unity. Every move must exhibit unity which is easily tested by summarizing the parts of a move into a simple clear sentence and by matching thematically the opening and closing statements. Unity ensures that the move will not fragment in consciousness, a phenomenon usually caused by alternating the focus or traveling the idea. Alteration in focus occurs when the preacher shifts from a past-tense look at Scripture to a present-tense view of our world, or when a contrapuntal is too strong, overcoming the statement idea. An idea travels when the opening and the closing statements match (1987: 49-50).

If a sermon is to reshape the faith consciousness of the people of God, every move will also exhibit varied points of view. Consciousness for modern men and women is perspectival, argues Buttrick. Hence, if preaching is to fit into the consciousness of twentieth-century people in a natural way, it too must be perspectival. Since point of view governs the style of preaching, one must be aware of differences in point of view and know how to employ different perspectives or stances in preaching. There are several categories of point-of-view. Stance is the spatial (speaking while lying on your back beneath a pine tree) or temporal (speaking in present time) position from which one speaks. Orientation is the direction of our intending (turning in our speech toward some place or time in the past) or aimed consciousness. Distance, which is measured in consciousness, is spatial (speaking of a starving African child seen on a TV screen across the room) or temporal (speaking of a past event as if immediate), emotional or attitudinal. Focal field, which is spatial or temporal, is like a camera lens that can be widened (looking at our world) or narrowed (looking at American policy in Nicaragua). Lens depth is the level of self-involvement expressed in the point-of-view. Focal depth refers to how far we see into what we are observing. It may be simply a surface impression, or may penetrate into the feelings and thoughts of a person (1987: 58-61).

There are a cluster of general rules to follow when creating moves. Preachers must learn to control point-of-view within a move, if they wish the congregation to truly hear the sermon. Since contemporary congregations are highly impressionable, a point-of-view must be established early in the move, specifically within the first three sentences. And the point-of-view must be maintained for the duration of the move. While changes in point-of-view will occur from move to move, "within a move we will wish to be disciplined" (1987: 62). Also, within a move, the preacher must maintain one particular stance and orientation lest the move splits and fails to form in consciousness. "Sudden shifts in stance, orientation, or distance will so effect language in consciousness as to fragment moves or bewilder congregations" (1987: 63).

Of course, there are some exceptions to these general rules. While it is possible to establish a moving stance or orientation at the start of a move by alerting the congregation with a cue sentence, one cannot begin a move with a fixed stance and then attempt to establish movement. Also, minor shifts in focal field, lens depth, and focal depth are manageable within a move, if the congregation is provided with appropriate cues. Further, while we can speak about different attitudes, as a general rule, the preacher's attitudinal point-of-view, if expressed, must not shift during a move unless the congregation is notified. Of course, the preacher should not voice an attitude that is not truly his for preachers are not actors on a stage but persons who share a common humanity with the congregation (1987: 63-64).

This notion of point-of-view is complex. Yet, it's a gift that we can learn to use. Variable points-of-view must characterize our sermons, even as it does everyday speaking. Generally speaking, the preacher establishes perspective early in the move and shifts in perspective occur from move to move rather than within an individual move. Indeed, each move expresses a single controlled perspective. Buttrick gives substantive attention to the matter of point-of-view because "point-of-view in language can serve the cause of human transformation" (1987: 65).

Buttrick rejects the approach of the older homiletic that preached categorical "points" joined by transitional paragraphs. "Though categorical sermons are intrinsically easy for preachers to jot down," says Buttrick, "they are intrinsically tedious for congregations" (1987: 115). Transitional sections are unnecessary when sermons are regarded as sequences of ideas or "moves." When putting moves together, what's needed is a way to keep the moves distinct so that there is structural toughness yet they need to be connected so that there is logical coherence. "Congregations are remarkably logical," asserts Buttrick. "Therefore, as preachers, we must pay attention to connective logic and be sure that such logic forms in congregational consciousness" (1987: 71).

Within a sermon, groups of moves may form a logical "set." In the following series of five moves of a sermon, the first three moves form a set and the last two form a set (1987: 75):

Be honest: We are all sinners.
But, good news, in Jesus Christ we are forgiven.
So, guess what? We can live in a new way.
Well, don't you want to tell your neighbor?
By the spread of the gospel, God redeems the world.

When dealing with sets like this, one needs to define the

set as a set and join the sets. To define sets the preacher can vary the starts and then use repetition like a refrain prior to the closure of both moves. Another strategy is to rehearse the ideas in the three sets prior to the closure of the third move. Unlike sequential moves, when joining sets, the connection will require a good deal of force. "The closure of a final move in a set will probably require several sentences," writes Buttrick, "and the opening of a following move will have to be equally emphatic—perhaps using five sentences to establish the move statement" (1987: 77).

As noted earlier, the reason the start of a move is so difficult to design is that it carries so much freight. It must focus consciousness, display connective logic, indicate point-of-view, and establish mood. Mood refers to the emotional tone of the sermon. Although emotion has been sadly neglected by many contemporary preachers who wish to avoid the errors of emotionalism, a lack of emotion is unnatural and unrelated to the urgency of the gospel of liberation through Jesus Christ. "Yes, we must reject all false, put-on emotion," says Buttrick, "but we must not turn from emotion per se" (1987: 78). In sum, the first three sentences of a move will carry the freight of content, connective logic, perspective, and mood.

4. Preaching and Framework. In writing of framework, Buttrick has two essential homiletical moves in mind: introductions and conclusions. Introductions provide focus like a camera lens by bringing a particular subject into vision against a backdrop of a larger field of meaning. Like a camera lens, focus serves a twofold purpose: "Locating a whole field of meaning, and isolating some particular feature within the field of meaning (usually connected with a first move)" (1987: 84). Practically speaking, the introduction sets up the sermon so that the first move may begin. The critical factor is avoiding introductions that are too general and hence unrelated to the first move or too particular and thus irrelevant to the whole sermon. The main test of a good introduction is its ability to facilitate a smooth, natural move into the body of the sermon.

Introductions should be designed with care and discipline. They should not give away the goods of the sermon before it begins. Also, they should not be too long, since they merely function to focus. Indeed, as a general rule, "introductions may run between seven and twelve sentences in length" (1987: 95). Further, introductions should not be too short since it takes a congregation at least two or three sentences to adjust to our speech patterns, four to six sentences to establish focus, and a single sentence to make a firm closure to the introduction. Moreover, they must stop so that the last words of an introduction come to a crisp, clear, conclusion. "The longest pause in the delivery of the sermon," says Buttrick, "will usually occur immediately following an introduction and before the body of a sermon begins" (1987: 87). Next, the middle six or eight sentences of an introduction do the work of focusing on a single issue, theme, mood, or field of meaning. Finally, if the sermon speaks of scripture, the introduction should include a reference to Scripture yet it should not be a labored documentation.

In addition to focusing consciousness, introductions provide a hermeneutical orientation that indicates to the congregation what is being discussed and how to listen. While the old dictum that sermons need to begin close to home, is not entirely trustworthy. "An introduction," writes Buttrick, "ought to establish shared consciousness between a preacher and congregation in which some image or idea may become focal" (1987: 92). Hence, I and you language is to be avoided because it does not draw preacher and people together into a shared consciousness.

After outlining a general approach to introductions, Buttrick names some pulpit conventions to avoid. Step-down introductions (first talking about Paul, then talking about Corinth, and finally talking about the Eucharist in the Corinthian Church) require too many shifts in point-of-view to focus congregational consciousness and irritate the hearers. Also, tangential remarks and intrusions cannot be tolerated in introductions for they disrupt focus and leave the congregation struggling for focus. Another convention to avoid are oblique remarks that are attempts to create suspense. They should be avoided for they too fail to focus consciousness. Yet another strategy to avoid is personal illustrations. Personal experiences in the introduction split the focus. "As a preacher," writes Buttrick, "you are attempting at the outset of a sermon to focus congregational consciousness on an image, or an idea.... But, by speaking of yourself, inevitably the congregation will focus on you" (1987: 94). Finally, humor is another common feature of sermon introductions to avoid. There are two difficulties with humor in introductions: first, the humor is usually totally unrelated to the focus of the sermon which the introduction seeks to introduce; and second, since the gospel speaks of Christ crucified for us, humor at the start of a sermon tends to trivialize the seriousness of the Christian faith (1987: 95).

Introductions give focus to consciousness and provide hermeneutical orientation. They demand disciplined language that is terse, visual, and focal. Preachers should write them out and learn them well. "The trick in preparing an introduction may be to put yourself in the place of your people" (1987: 96).

Conclusions, on the other hand, serve to bring the sermon to the point of intention and then stop. Conclusions do not introduce new ideas and they are not long; they are five to eight sentences at most. What's critical for a conclusion is that it fixes intention. Since sermons intend to do something, the preacher must determine what a particular sermon is trying to do before he or she can prepare a conclusion. Often the intention of the biblical text is discerned and then incorporated into the conclusion of the sermon. At other times the key question may be discerning what the sermon intends to do. "Each conclusion will fulfill some different intention," writes Buttrick, "and each, therefore, may be different in shape, and mood and language" (1987: 100).

The critical issue is how to bring a sermon to a conclusion and yet ensure a lasting impact from the sermon. Buttrick suggests that the first two or three sentences of a conclusion must establish a reflective consciousness "without tipping off a congregation to the fact that a conclusion is taking place" (1987: 101). One strategy is to create a conclusion that draws together parts of a sermon and thus echoes images and phrases of the sermon's moves.

Another strategy is to create a conclusion that fulfills the aim of the sermon by functioning as a natural outcome of the sermonic material. In the last three sentences of a conclusion a sense of ending is expressed by some form of repetition or by a terse last sentence. Indeed, the last sentence of the conclusion, which is short, and unencumbered with adjectival or clausal modifiers, simply stops (1987: 101-102).

There are several conventions that are problematic. Ending a sermon with a question is problematic because evidence suggests that congregations delete such questions from consciousness the moment they are asked. A better strategy is to create a picture in consciousness of someone doing what the sermon wants God's people to do. Another popular strategy that should be avoided is ending a sermon with a quotation. The conclusion is a direct talk situation that demands a high level of eye contact and high degree of intimacy. A further convention to avoid involves returning to the introduction. It may provide satisfaction but it stifles response to the sermon by creating a closed circle in consciousness in which nothing more needs to be said or done. "If we wish sermons to move and motivate, to transform lives, we will avoid conclusions that turn back and reprise introductory material" (1987: 105). Yet another convention to avoid is rhythmic intensifications that strive for emotional impact. More than one repetition in a conclusion may enable the preacher to feel something but the congregation will not feel in the same way. A final strategy often employed by preachers is personal testimony. While personal testimony may be appropriate at earlier points of the sermon, it is most inappropriate in a conclusion because it leaves the congregation with a consciousness of the preacher rather than the gospel (1987: 106). As a general rule, when creating a conclusion, shun vague categorical labels and instead use direct, simple, concrete images. "Conclusions are acts of obedience; we are doing what is intended. They are practical matters; we stop" (1987: 109).

5. *Preaching as Imaging*. Images and metaphors are central to understanding the function and operation of illustrations and examples in preaching. Since analogy is the language of faith, analogical language is critical to preaching. By means of metaphor, simile and image we speak about God's likeness to us. Of course, we qualify our analogies with the language of amplification and denial in order to say that God is much more than our likeness and to signal that God's ways are not our ways. "Faith is formed in a nexus of image, symbol, metaphor, and ritual," writes Buttrick. "Therefore, the language of preaching is essentially metaphorical" (1987: 125).

Like metaphor, illustrations and examples are also native to the language of faith and hence preaching. The preacher essentially draws examples from the shared experiences of the congregation whereas illustrations are imported from outside of the common consciousness of the congregation. Both examples and illustrations are crucial to preaching because they can bridge time, build models in consciousness, and compress blocks of meaning into a coherent system (1987: 128).

Examples serve many functions. They establish the truth of statements by showing that they correspond to lived life. Also, examples shape analogies as when we liken God's forgiveness to parental forgiveness. Further, examples portray a slice of life for study. Of course, examples must be used in a disciplined manner. First, in sermons, examples may be brief or enlarged but they must be controlled and not overdeveloped lest they fail to express the shared experience of the congregation. Second, examples will convey how things affect us or how we act in our daily lives. Third, when using an example in preaching, it is best to carefully design it, including actual concrete description so that the example will be real to life. Fourth, within a single move only one example should be used unless one is trying to establish that some statement is true to life in which case a chain of no more than three examples may be used. Fifth, the preacher will locate examples within his or her own memory bank. One simply turns toward memory and recalls experiences of what actually happens in life. However, these recollections should be assessed to ensure that they are true to life (1987: 128-133).

Unlike examples, illustrations are imported. They include short quotes, briefly described scenes, action episodes, pictures, stories, and bits of dialogue. But again, illustrations must be used with care. There are three criteria for evaluating illustrations. First, there must be a clear similarity between the illustration and the sermon content. Second, there should be a parallel between the shape of the illustration and the structure of the content. Third, the illustration must be appropriate; it must fit the content. "If illustrations function within moves," writes Buttrick, "they will be governed by the content, shape, and intention of a move, and must fit into the move's point-of-view" (1987: 135).

There are several ground rules for the use of illustrations. (1) unlike examples, illustrations may not be multiplied within a move. Indeed, only one illustration may be used in a single move for multiple illustrations weaken analogy and make understanding difficult. (2) Illustrations must fit the content of the move which they will do if they exhibit a clear analogy with the content of the move, if they parallel the structure of the content, and if they are appropriate to the content. (3) Illustrations must not overpower the strength of the move and throw the sermon out of balance. Instead, they should relate to the move so as to support its content rather than detract from the content of a move. (4) Illustrations must also coincide with the positive or negative character of the move. Thus, an illustration of lovelessness will not match a move that is urging love for one another. (5) Illustrations must relate to the basic model of the text. Thus, a sermon on the parable of the sower should relate to its fields of imagery, such as agriculture, house plants, growth in general, and few to many multiplications. (6) Illustrations of some length should be avoided for they will probably detract from the meaning of the move instead of functioning to illustrate it (1987: 135-141).

There are several conventions associated with illustrations that are questionable. First, regarding the habit of using personal illustrations in a sermon, Buttrick says: "To be blunt, there are virtually no good reasons to talk about ourselves from the pulpit" (1987: 142). Usually personal illustrations throw more light on the preacher's personality than the sermon's content. Also, avoid peppering the sermon with quotes that require the congregation to adjust from the preacher's oral pattern of speech to the prose material's syntax. Further, we can only draw on a limited repertoire of biblical illustrations because today's congregation is not well acquainted with scripture. Finally, regarding humor, there are two rules: first, congregations should laugh only when the preacher has good reasons for wanting them to laugh; and second, "if you are naturally funny, your problem is control; if you are not naturally funny, do not try it!" (1987: 147).

Since illustrations are intended to illustrate, preachers are encouraged to delete extra agendum. "Illustrations must be pared down, the point of analogy heightened, and, as much as possible, the shape of an illustration made to match the structure of thought in a move" (1987: 147). To strip away extraneous fat, preachers should write out illustrations in advance, limiting them to about a dozen sentences at most since compressed images are more powerful. Also, it should be recognized at the outset that not every move will have an illustration, yet when used they must be shaped into the move, "knitting them into content with care, yet, at the same time, protecting the strong starts and finishes of moves" (1987: 148). As a general rule, illustrations and ideas are joined together by weaving illustration and content together, avoiding obtrusive introductions to illustrations and dangling at the end of the illustration. Finally, the preacher should give credit for an imported illustration, not by endless name-dropping, but by unobtrusively indicating to the congregation that it is not his or her material (1987: 149-150).

Since sermons are for the forming of faith in consciousness, Buttrick proposes the idea of an image grid. Whereas older homiletics employed illustrations and examples to support points, he suggests that sermons build a faith world in consciousness by means of images, metaphors, illustrations, and examples. Therefore, the appropriateness of an illustration must be tested by how it relates to a particular move and how it interrelates with the whole sermon. "What makes a good sermon is not one single illustration, but a gridwork of interacting images, examples, and illustrations" (1987: 153). Thus, in the initial stage of sermon preparation, one simply lists a series of sentences on a page to form an outline. At this point, it would be premature to gather images, examples, and illustrations for they may dominate the thought structure of a sermon. "As a rule, then," cautions Buttrick, "it will always be better to develop each of the move sentences in a sermon" (1987: 154). Later, and only after each of the move sentences has been elaborated so that one has some sense of how ideas will form, one can begin to gather material. "Initially, the process does involve a kind of brainstorming," writes Buttrick, "a free associating that involves dredging up out of memory half-recalled material, stuff we have seen or read or heard" (1987: 155). Next, after brainstorming each move of the sermon and after listing possible images, examples, and illustrations for each move of the whole sermon, one can begin choosing and selecting illustrations for a single move but always with the whole sermon in view. "In effect, we will gather stuff for a whole sermon and then," says Buttrick, "with an eye to structural design, select with care" (1987: 156).

Thus, Buttrick proposes designing an interacting image grid by means of reprise, refrain, and interrelating illustrations. Ultimately, the image grid reflects the fact that sermons are intended to form faith consciousness. "Preachers are not poets," says Buttrick, "but they should have a poet's eye. More, preachers should take delight in putting words and images together as they build a world for faith" (1987: 170).

6. Language and Preaching. Buttrick is critical of both the communication and expressive models of language theory because they are uncongenial to a theology of Word. He prefers to define the language of preaching as "a connotative language used with theological precision" (1987: 185). The language of preaching is simple. It must be ordinary language, the common shared vocabulary of the congregation. He estimates that the typical seminary graduate has a vocabulary of around 12,000 words while the average member of a church has one of about 7,500 words. But since everyone has a collection of around 2,500 technical words and local expressions, "the common shared vocabulary of a congregation will consist of about 5,000 words" (1987: 188). Also, the language of preaching is highly connotative. While denotative language is fine for business, it is inadequate for preaching because it spends its time talking about things; it is observational, objective and lacks personal involvement. What preaching requires is connotative language for sermons intended to form faith powerfully in congregational consciousness by combining phenomenal imagery with imaginative syntax and metaphorical language (1987: 192). Moreover, the connotative language of preaching must be theologically appropriate. He does not encourage the use of in-house religious terms like redemption, salvation, and sanctification for they simply "drape discourse in an aura of old-time religious respectability" (1987: 194). What he means by theologically apt is that it is not appropriate to speak about the "kingdom of God" in individualistic terms as a personal possession when, biblically speaking, the kingdom of God is a social reality. According to Buttrick, "we must speak the language of common image and metaphor, but do so with theological wisdom" (1987: 194).

Two additional criteria are to be used to assess the language of preaching. First, the language of preaching is intended to form in congregational consciousness. Hence, preachers will need to check their private and personal expressions of the faith and life against the measure of their social and public usefulness. While preachers seek a freshness of expression, "the images we choose and use must work in congregational consciousness" (1987: 195). Second, the language of preaching must serve the moves in a sequence of sermon scenarios. "The language of preaching is not a language *per se*, but is always a language doing a particular move" (1987: 195). The above five yardsticks, then, are the norms Buttrick offers for assessing the language of preaching. No wonder he describes preaching as "a considered craft" (1987: 193).

Buttrick rejects the notion that preachers should develop their own style. Instead, he argues that, as unique individuals, preachers already have a unique way of speaking. The real issue is to bend our style so that it may serve the twin purposes of representing the gospel and serving congregational consciousness. To that end, Buttrick believes it is helpful to be aware of three components of style. First, preachers should not fear the sounds of words. For example, when speaking of cruelty, preachers should not hesitate to employ words with harsh guttural sounds. However, the sounds of words are governed by rules. If the sounds used do not fall within the range of the speaker's ordinary speech patterns, they will draw attention to themselves rather than serving the speaker's purpose. So when using the sounds of words, speakers should not alter their own syntax. Also, the sounds of the words should function "to serve the meaning we are attempting to shape" (1987: 207).

Another component of style is cadenced and rhythmic speech. Cadences are rhythms caused by syntax or rhythms formed from the sound of words. They vary according to subject matter. Repetition ("God calls us back. God calls us back to the faith of our founders"), doublets ("Our nation is great and good, holy and happy") and triadic clauses ("We believe in God, we believe in God's Word, and we believe in doing God's will") are the most common sources of syntactical rhythms. Generally speaking, different cadences should be employed for every move. Rhythms are also created by syllables in words and by stresses on syllables in attempt to shape words to match ideas. For example, "Click your heels and skip a little" is better than "Click your heels and run a little." Or, "Life's more fun than you know" is better than "Life's more pleasant than you know." Conversational forms like exclamations, questions, direct address, repetition, inversion, synecdoche, personification, and apostrophe are also components of style that are part of everyone's conversational repertoire (1987: 209-211).

Since faith comes from hearing, preachers must strive to be heard. Unfortunately, congregational consciousness, which can retain large amounts of information, often instantly erases like a tape recorder. Research shows that only 35% of a reasonably good sermon is retained in congregational consciousness. If preachers wish to achieve at least 60% retention, they should avoid some common language pitfalls. First, there are some words that are problematic. Demonstrative pronouns (this, that, these, those) should not be used to begin a sentence since such sentences are instantly deleted from congregational consciousness. As a rule we should avoid using two or more "it" sentence in sequence. Intensifiers such as "very," "really," and "indeed" should be avoided. Delaying words like "actually" and "however" are deemed dreadful in speaking. Sentences that begin with enumeration will be deleted from consciousness. "Thus" and "therefore" are never used in ordinary conversation so they should not be used in sermons. While all of the above examples may seem minor, they are not for the issue is hearing. "If certain words or phrases obstruct our hearing the gospel, then, obviously, we will excise them from our sermons," says Buttrick (1987: 213).

Second, there are some syntactical problems that should be noted. Doublets in sentences should be avoided. Take the following sentence: "God wants peace and justice." The problem here is that two different things are being said at the same time. "Virtually all doublet sentences," says Buttrick, "will instantly erase; they will not function in consciousness" (1987: 213). When preachers employ sentences with triple words—"God wants peace, and justice, and perfect obedience"—they literally irritate the congregation. Syntactical repetitions should be limited to one or two in a single sermon.

Third, there are certain expressions that cause difficulties. Slang phrases like "uptight" or "He's boss" are not to be used unless the people regularly employ them. Religious clichés like "washed in the blood" or "Brothers and sisters" should be avoided since they only serve to alienate faith from life. Special subcultural words and phrases like "bottom line" or "opinion shaper" need not creep into sermons.

Although Buttrick considers general guidelines of little use, he relents and mentions a few that point the preacher in the direction of good sermon style. First, preaching language is concrete; it avoids conceptual terms like "goals," "relationships," "situations," or "desires." Second, sermons use verbs that give color or visual character and verbs that give precision or distinctive meaning. Thus, expressions like "we peer," "we peek," and "we stare" are preferred to "we look." Third, the weakest word in preaching is the adjective. We rarely use adjectives in everyday conversation. So he suggests that we should never use adjectives for effect and use them only when necessary. Fourth, pronouns are fine to use, especially "we" and "our" and "us." However, since we should use language that connects the preacher with the congregation, preaching should avoid "you and I," "you and me." Also, "I" is always dangerous when used alone, the word "you" is most suitable if used in this way: "What were you going to do?" Fifth, in general, preaching employs the present tense, active voice, and simple short sentences (1987: 217-220).

Buttrick insists that preachers can learn to work with words. Speaking is a craft that must be learned, not an art. Preachers can learn much about using words effectively from books, poets, novelists, and dramatists. "We will learn more about language from poets, novelists, and dramatists," says Buttrick, "than from reading chapters on sermon style penned by some professor of homiletics" (1987: 220-221).

Buttrick's Approach Implemented

"Vine, Branches, Grapes" is a sermon based on the text of John 15:1-8 and preached at the North Fresno MB Church in 1994. It is reproduced here to demonstrate that Buttrick's approach is understandable and capable of adaptation by today's preachers. Please read the biblical text prior to the reading of the sermon.

Sermon
"Vine, Branches, Grapes"

Several years ago, while studying in Europe, my wife and I had the privilege of worshiping in a wide variety of church buildings in England and Germany. In many of these old church buildings we came across the vine, the branches, and the grapes. Painted on walls, carved into communion tables, or set in stained glass. Somewhere there was apt to be a picture of the vine, the branches and the grapes. Perhaps the only way to understand the mystery of our life in Christ is to look at pictures. Jesus is the vine and we are the branches.

1.

At the outset, notice: the image of the vine and the branches is true to life. If we're honest, we'll have to admit that cut off from Christ the vine, we're pretty helpless as God's people. We can't make it as Christians with only common sense and a subscription to *Psychology Today*. Cut off from Christ the vine, we soon grow weary in our well doing. We can decide to love by forgiving the one who has wounded us and we can decide to maintain a relationship with our offender in spite of the pain, but soon we find our love withering away in the heat of everyday life. We can determine to be charitable, to give to the indigent poor, to contribute to a worthy cause, but when the bills pile up and the advertisements beckon, we cut our percentages, we trim our donations. We can decide to serve and work with others on a community project, to give ourselves away, but when the going gets tough, we throw in the towel and call it quits. One year in the San Joaquin Valley the peaches were especially plentiful. The fruit was big and juicy. It was one of the best crops in memory. While harvesting the crop, a picker noticed a limb that had fallen from a tree. Its fruit was rotten and shriveled. Because the limb was detached from the tree, it was no longer producing good fruit. Look, if we are honest, apart from Christ we are pretty helpless. Cut off from Christ, we have no ability to love, give, and serve. Separated from the vine, our good intentions quickly wither and die.

2.

But listen: We are joined to the Vine. Our lives are rooted in Jesus Christ. Every Christian and every church has grown out of the Christ-event. We are connected to Jesus Christ by faith. Think back through the years. Your faith comes to you from someone—a parent, a friend, a pastor, a co-worker, or maybe the author of a book. And his or her faith comes from someone, all the way back through time and space to Jesus Christ. The fact is our lives spring from Jesus Christ. By faith we are connected to the Vine. We are organically, biologically, anatomically connected to Jesus Christ. There's an old church history book in the seminary library. It contains a picture of the Christian Family tree. Vines, representing the apostles, sprout from the cross; branches, representing the many Christian denominations, spread through the ages and into our own century. We are joined to Jesus Christ. Thanks to God we are organically related to Christ by faith. We are joined to the Vine.

3.

Now let's confess: Christ also prunes our lives. Christ shapes our character as Christians. As we gather together week after week, we hear the word of Christ and the word of Christ trims us and gives us our identity. When we gather together, we learn of Jesus Christ. We hear sermons and Sunday School lessons. We get involved in study circles and discussion groups. Sometimes the Bible is the hammer that breaks our hardened hearts, the double-edged sword that divides asunder our thoughts and intents, or the mirror that reflects our sins. At other times, the Bible is the seed that generates new life within us, the water that washes us, or the milk and the meat that nourishes us. We are clipped and trimmed by God's word. Drive through the San Joaquin Valley of California in the spring of the year and you will be amazed at what you see in the vineyards. The vines are gnarled stumps. You will see hundreds of acres of thick stalks, a little longer than a person's arm. They don't look like much. They are rough, ugly, and unseemly. At the end of each row lay piles of trash, discarded branches, unnecessary appendages cut off from the vine. So it is with us—Christ prunes us. Maybe our situation is like the old woman who, while ruthlessly cutting back a rosebush, muttered to her rose bushes, "You want beauty, don't you? You want beauty, don't you?" Jesus Christ shapes our lives. He gives us our identity. Christ trims us. God's word prunes our lives and we are formed and reformed by Christ the Vine.

4.

Now look at the fruit: Grapes, clusters of grapes are produced because we are joined to the Vine. Joined to Jesus Christ, the harvest is sure to be abundant. It is our calling to bear fruit and fruit bearing is the sign of our abiding in the Vine. Look at what is happening through the church all around the world. We are not talking about fulfilling our human potential. No, we are talking about our likeness to Jesus Christ the Vine. We are talking about love, service, and joy. We are talking about MBMSI with an annual budget of almost 5 million dollars and almost 200 missionaries and their families dispersed around the world loving other people in the style of our Lord, which represents a lot of giving and loving. We are talking about 177 MBBS graduates placed in ministry during the past 6 years alone, some 1,070 in the past 40 years—pastors, counselors, chaplains, teachers, missionaries, and marketplace ministers—scattered all around the globe, which represents a lot of giving and serving. We are talking about MCC International with its annual budget of almost 50 million dollars and over 900 voluntary workers around the planet, which represents a lot of giving and joy to the world. Once upon a time, an old monk, a wine taster, had a superb definition of vintage: "It's vintage," he says, "when you've got so much you have to give it away!" Since we are joined to Jesus Christ the Vine we have so much love that we have to give it away. Yes, there is pruning, trimming, and cutting. But the net result is clusters and clusters of grapes. Joined to Jesus the harvest is abundant. We produce fruit because we are connected to the Vine.

5.

So what's at stake? The gardener's reputation is at stake. Our fruitfulness brings glory and praise to God the Father who owns the vineyard. God is glorified and praised when we remain connected to the Vine and bear much fruit. One church expresses its purpose like this: "Man's chief end is to glorify God, and enjoy him forever." The heart of biblical piety is the desire to give glory to God in everything we say and do. We glorify God when we bow down before him in praise and adoration out of gratefulness for what he has done for us in Jesus Christ. We glorify our God when we dedicate ourselves to the Great Commission, sharing the gospel with our friends and expressing our concern for their eternal destiny. We glorify God when we feed the hungry, clothe the naked, and visit the sick in prison. A well-known African American evangelist is fond of saying, "if you want to find out what is happening in heaven you should be able to check out the church." As imperfect as we are, our acts of love, service, and mercy remind people that God is at work, making all things new. The fruit is important because the Gardener's reputation is at stake. Our fruitfulness is a sign that we belong to Jesus Christ the Vine.

Now here are two images. The first image is a branch, cut off from the vine, withering away in the hot afternoon sun, ready to be gathered up and thrown into the fire. The second image is a branch, connected to the vine, nicely trimmed but laden with clusters of grapes. Put both pictures in your mind. "You are the vine, and we are the branches. Keep us abiding in you."

Buttrick's Method Evaluated

1. Strength of Buttrick's Strategy. Perhaps the most noteworthy strength of Buttrick's strategy is its use of rhetoric. As Thomas G. Long writes, "the most exciting aspect of Buttrick's book is its return to 'Christian rhetoric'" (1987: 4). By definition, rhetoric is concerned with how human beings actually hear and grasp meaning. No wonder Buttrick notes things like the short attention span of today's congregation and as a consequence suggests that a sermon will be twenty minutes long with four minutes for each move and a maximum of five or six sequenced subjects in each sermon. He asserts that his preaching strategy stands squarely on Paul's homiletic fact of life: "Faith comes by hearing." He argues that a sermon can be structured to shape the faith consciousness of its listeners. He believes that preachers can shape words, phrases, images, illustrations, and sequenced scenarios to affect the faith consciousness of a congregation. For Buttrick, sermon strategy is a theological issue for a homiletic method concerned with "how to present the gospel message to an emerging quite different human consciousness" (1994: 80). If twentieth-century homiletics, under the sway of the biblical theology movement, severed itself from rhetoric, Buttrick re-connects homiletics with rhetoric, arguing that we must "learn to shape the language of speaking so that people will more readily grasp meaning and believe" (1994: 67). Thomas G. Long says,

> Buttrick compels us to think long and hard about what is happening inside the heads of listeners as we preach. He has a high view of the power of language and form to make things happen, and he is convinced, correctly, that a sermon

shaped one-way forms faith quite differently from
a sermon shaped another way (1989: 103).

In short, Buttrick's unwillingness to separate theology
and homiletics is commendable.

A second strength of Buttrick's strategy concerns the
way the biblical text is treated in preaching. His approach
focuses more on how the language of the text functions
and less on the meaning of its content. In Buttrick's phenomenological approach, scripture provides a rhetorical
model for preaching. John S. McLure labels Buttrick's
way of handling the biblical text "transpositional." By this
term he means that the sermon "strives in some way to do
rhetorically what the Scripture does or 'intends' rhetorically" (1991: 29-30). McLure notes that it is presently a
most popular new trend in homiletics for many consider it
to be a more thoroughly biblical approach to preaching.
Leander Keck is a case in point. In his discussion of biblical preaching, Keck insists that "preaching is biblical
when it imparts a Bible-shaped word in a Bible-like way"
(1978: 106). For example, Buttrick studies the biblical story of the ten lepers in Luke 17:11-19 and concludes that
the passage functions as a call to worship. Therefore, he
prepares a sketch of a sermon that will also function as
call to worship (1987: 340, 346). Buttrick's approach replicates the intentional language of the biblical text.

A third strength of Buttrick's strategy is that it bridges
the traditional gap between exegetical method and
homiletic method. Homiletic textbooks often encourage
the preacher to begin designing a sermon only after having completed the exegetical work on a text and having
formulated a theme sentence. For some, the discontinuity
between arriving at a message and designing a sermon is
accentuated by the suggestion that the preacher take-a-
break between the two exercises. Buttrick observes that
the crucial shift from the study of the text to the conception of the sermon is often not discussed, giving the
preacher the impression that one moves from Bible to sermon as if by magic (Fee, 1983: 133). Instead, Buttrick insists that as the preacher translates, studies, and considers

the text "the structure of the biblical passage forms a contemporary structure of meaning in his consciousness" (1987: 89). In this way, every sermon is preached from a contemporary structure of meaning prompted by the study of scripture. The preacher moves almost unconsciously from exegesis to a field of understanding and then to the production of a sermon. We preach from a contemporary structure of understanding in consciousness which is a kind of "middle ground" between exegesis and sermon; it helps to bridge the text to sermon gap found in other treatments of homiletics.

A fourth strength of Buttrick's strategy is its attention to the movement of language and the logic of movement in both biblical texts and sermonic forms. He insists that biblical passages are more like film-clips from motion pictures than static, still-life snapshots. Biblical passages "travel along with the give and take of lively conversation, moving from one idea to another" (1994: 83). For example, Hebrews 12:1-3 travels by visual logic, featuring the metaphor of a marathon and moving from a crowd of past champions to runners getting ready to race, to a pace-setting victorious Christ. Since sermons are movements of thought from beginning to end, they are developed like sequenced scenarios. Meaning is structural and structure is shaped by movement of thought or image or event as we journey into truth. Buttrick's approach is convincing at this point. Indeed, preachers should favor mobile structures as opposed to categorical point-making sermons based on propositional truths distilled from allegedly static, still-life biblical text.

A fifth strength of Buttrick's strategy relates to his contention that preaching aims at communal consciousness. He rightly underscores the fact that biblical texts were addressed to communal, and not merely individual, consciousness. Scripture was written for a faith community and deals with shared meaning. Therefore, as interpreters of the text preachers do not ask "What does the text say to me?" but "What does the text say to our faith-consciousness?" (Fee 1989: 3-13).

2. *The Weakness of Buttrick's Strategy*. The first weakness in Buttrick's strategy relates to the question of a preacher's ability to master and use it in weekly sermon preparation. As Richard Eslinger aptly states: "The success of this distinctive approach to preaching largely depends on the degree to which it is comprehensible and adaptable for the preacher who is a novice to the system" (1987: 162). Even if one accepts Buttrick's critique of the older homiletic, is it possible to implement his approach after a careful reading of his strategy? Thomas G. Long is not optimistic about the prospects of its use by students and pastors. In a critical review of Buttrick's book, he writes: "The book will surely be criticized for providing a model of sermon development and analysis too cumbersome and labyrinthine for students and pastors to master and use in the weekly press of sermon creation" (1987: 3). However, another reviewer of Buttrick's book, while acknowledging that it is not "a lighthearted primer for preachers," suggests that "it is a serious and occasionally ponderous work intended for homileticians, theologians, and those preachers most serious about their preaching task" (Mohler 1987: 40). Others, such as Craig Loscalzo, indicate that Buttrick informed members of the Academy of Homiletics in 1988 that his book was not intended for preachers or seminarians at the master's level. "He said," writes Loscalzo, "his intention was to provoke teachers of preaching and the field of homiletics to rethink approaches, that is, paradigms" (1992: 56). Loscalzo encourages preachers to look elsewhere if they are looking for a how-to-write-a-sermon book.

A second weakness of Buttrick's method relates to the stated goal of the sermon as communication that forms faith in consciousness. Thomas G. Long rightly questions the rigidity of Buttrick's approach. He asks, "Do ideas really get formed in human consciousness in the way Buttrick claims they do?" (1987: 104). Buttrick wants every move to be shaped in a very precise way so that faith consciousness is finally formed by the sermon. Each move has an opening statement, followed by a development, and then a closure that restates the idea. "What Buttrick has done," observes Long, "is to produce an abstract schematic description of one way of thinking and to declare that process as normative for each section of a sermon" (1987: 104). The point is that there are likely other ways in which faith consciousness is formed in people. Buttrick cannot assume that each and every hearer is essentially the same when it comes to forming faith consciousness. Moreover, in order to understand how faith forms in human consciousness, he analyzes people in the world instead of asking how language functions for people being-saved in community in the world. Long says, "He moves to a rarefied notion of how language forms in consciousness generally—in everybody, everywhere, always" (O'Day 1993: 183).

A third weakness of Buttrick's approach is related to the way it treats the historical and cultural dimensions of the biblical text. Since the language of the text and its performative function is the critical piece in a Buttrick-style sermon, the historical and cultural background of the text receives short shrift. Indeed, John S. McClure considers this weakness to be the principal problem with the phenomenological approach to preaching. He notes that it is a sermonic strategy that tends to avoid references to factual and historical details in the text. McLure writes:

> Congregations hear stories and plots along with the intentions they express but are not invited to consider the veracity and meaning of what actually happened during Jesus' ministry. The good news is not what happened or even the early church's understanding of the meaning of what happened, but the way the biblical text "calls" readers to interact with it, with life, and with their own world (1991: 31).

In addition, the preacher who is pressured to produce a sermon every week, may be tempted to dismiss the time consuming work of historical criticism. And even when these observations have been made in study they may not find their way into the sermon.

A fourth weakness of Buttrick's approach relates to the form of the sermon. As noted, sermons shaped according to Buttrick's strategy, are conceived as "mobile structures." That is, the sermon is a "series of immediate thoughts, sequentially designed and imaged with technical skill so as to assemble in forming faith" (1981: 56). "But surely," writes Thomas Long, "sermons are more than a series of idea-laden boxcars moving down the track" (1987: 104).

A fifth weakness of Buttrick's approach concerns the fact that it renders some biblical texts unpreachable. He essentially argues that biblical texts must have a central intention, a narrative line, or a logic of movement, if they are to be preachable. Such a precondition inevitably rules out some biblical materials. Buttrick does not flinch from simply stating that some material does not belong in what he calls the "homiletic canon." Indeed, he peers at Psalms and Proverbs through his phenomenological lens and concludes that the psalms are intended as hymns of praise and the proverbs are designed to function as social wisdom. The language of the biblical psalms and proverbs do not want to be preached (1981: 55). Elsewhere, he asks: "Is the whole Bible a book that must be preached simply because it is the Bible and somebody has labeled it as the Word of God?" (1994: 11). Even more forcefully, he writes: "If there are passages which cannot be preached without launched expeditions into historical background or lengthy critical excursus, they may not belong in the homiletic 'canon' (Not all Scripture may want to be preached!)." (1981: 55). Thus, Buttrick's strategy is not applicable to those portions of the Bible that lack the logic and mobility required of a "moves" sermon.

Conclusion

I will compare and contrast the three homiletical strategies of Craddock, Lowry and Buttrick, paying special attention to their respective understandings of the sermon's definition, purpose, form, and preparation process. Also, the emphasis each gives to the listener will be compared and contrasted and the position that each homiletician takes on rational homiletics will be noted. Finally, the theological significance that each homiletician attaches to his homiletic method will be ascertained.

1. Questioning Rationalistic Homiletics. All three homileticians wish to divorce themselves in varying degrees from traditional methods of preaching. Fred Craddock is especially critical of deductive preaching that tends to move from general truth to particular application. In his view it is an approach that embraces several highly questionable presuppositions. First, it presumes that the sermon is fundamentally data about Scripture to be shared with passive listeners. Such a view of the function of scripture in preaching makes no room for the dynamic of God's Word. The Word of God is not simply the object of a preacher's analysis, but rather the subject of revelation; it is fundamentally God's revealing activity; it is primarily act and event. He reminds us that traditional preaching is as old as Aristotle. It involves a deductive movement downward which is a most unnatural mode of communication. He observes: "Looked at geographically, a three-point sermon on this pattern would take the congregation on three trips down hill, but who gets them to the top each time?" (1971: 54). Second, the traditional approach assumes an authoritarian foundation for preaching that is no longer appropriate in today's culture. It assumes that the preacher stands apart from and above the people in the things of the Spirit, creating a distance between pulpit and pew that violates the identification pastors must have with their people if the Word of God is to come alive in preaching. "No longer," writes Craddock, "can the preacher presuppose the general recognition of his authority as clergyman, or the authority of his institution, or the authority of the Scripture" (1971: 14). Third, the deductive model views the congregation as passive recipients of the message. "There is no democracy here, no dialogue, no listening by the speaker, no contributing by the hearer" (1971: 55). The traditional deductive approach to preaching is both methodologically and theologically bankrupt.

Lowry is equally critical of traditional forms of preaching. First, it is a homiletical form in which the presentation is deductive. The conclusion is announced in the introduction with the body of the sermon divided and particularized into three points, and finally reiterated in the conclusion. This homiletical form wrongly assumes that preaching consists primarily of "transmitting a set of complete ideas from one location to another via the 'conveyer belt' called speech" (Robinson 1990: 68). Second, the deductive approach to preaching assumes that divine revelation was given in propositions. However, the Christian revelation simply cannot be contained in propositional form, says Lowry. It is to a large extent non-propositional. "At best, propositional statements viewed formally can be no more than dead skeletons of what once was lived experience" (1985: 79). Third, the deductive approach essentially assumes that preaching is the ordering of ideas when in reality it is the ordering of experience (1985: 11-28).

David Buttrick is perhaps the most strident of the three in his criticism of what he calls the older homiletic. He questions it on three accounts. First, the older homiletic wrongly assumes that biblical passages are objects of contemplation. It treats biblical texts "as if they were still-life pictures full of things to isolate and talk about." Topics are distilled from chunks of scripture. What is discarded in the process, explains Buttrick, is "both narrative structure and, in non-narrative passages, the rhetoric of a structural movement" (1994: 82). Second, the older homiletic produces categorical point-making sermons which are intrinsically tedious for the congregation. Buttrick writes: "Categorical systems are easy, but only for the clergy.... they are hard to listen to in a congregation" (1994: 84). When we preach the gospel message, says Buttrick,

> We are not speaking some fixed Word of God truth that hangs before us like a poster and that we can discuss by pointing. No, as preachers we are journeying with our people into the mysteries of God, and journeying requires a very different homiletic method (1994: 84).

Third, the older homiletic presupposes a rationalistic scientific worldview that is quickly disappearing. It is now widely recognized that "reality is defined by consciousness" (1994: 79). What's needed, argues Buttrick, is new ways of preaching for an emerging new human consciousness.

2. Defining Homiletic Methods. In his earlier writings, Fred Craddock called his method "inductive" preaching, later however he dropped the use of this term (Wilson 1995: 214). After noting that everyone lives inductively, that even the incarnation itself is inductive, and that the sermon preparation process is inductive, Craddock asks: "Why not re-create with the congregation...[one's] inductive experience of coming to an understanding of the message of the text?" (1971: 125). By moving from particular to general, he maintains that the inductive approach helps to build anticipation in the listener as opposed to the boredom created by unpacking a thesis deductively in two or three points. Craddock does not use the expression "narrative preaching," except in his book *Overhearing the Gospel*, where he speaks about imaginative language requiring a carefully chosen structure to be effective. He writes:

> The shape of the communication is paramount in the business of effecting listener experience, and if the experience being sought is overhearing, the

structure most congenial and with greatest potential for effectiveness is narrative (1978: 135).

By contrast, Eugene Lowry frequently uses the term
"narrative" to describe his method. Indeed, he advocates
"a new image of the sermon" as "a homiletical plot, a narrative art form, a sacred story" (1980: 6). Since biblical
narrative already has its own plot, he does not utilize his
five step homiletical plot form in conjunction with biblical
narrative passages. Instead, he says, "the purpose of a narrative plot form is to make any sermon—life situational,
doctrinal or expositional—a narrative event" (1980: 76). In
a recent article, Lowry claims that he identifies himself
with those who are working primarily on the question of
"narrative sermonic shape" (O'Day 1993: 96). He goes on
to suggest that narrative homiletical form is an apt way to
label what he is advocating in preaching. Lowry notes a
technicality about his narrative sermons:

> One might point out that a plotted sermon
> moves with inductive process throughout approxi-
> mately three-fourths of the sermon until the deci-
> sive turn or reversal, at which point it flips over to
> deductive reasoning the rest of the way (O'Day
> 1993: 99).

David Buttrick cannot be called a narrative homiletician. He uses the term "narrative sermon" to refer to
preaching in the mode of immediacy. He writes: "In handling biblical narratives, preachers will be imitating a language of immediacy in which the movement of a plot
structures consciousness.... Of course, all narrative sermons will be moving toward the formation of reflective
consciousness" (1987: 335). Eugene Lowry notes Buttrick's concern for process, especially as expressed by his
nomenclature of moves. Then he compares his method
with Buttrick's saying, "I have often said that if you image
a sermon as a string of pearls, Buttrick would be interested primarily in the pearls; I am interested primarily in the

string" (O'Day 1993: 99-100). Instead of the term narrative or inductive, Buttrick uses the term "phenomenological" to describe his homiletical approach (1987: xii). While he refrains from identifying with the philosophical school of phenomenology, he states that the term is appropriate because he is primarily interested in the way language forms in consciousness. While commenting on the primary concern of his book *Homiletic,* he says: "I try to describe how sermons happen in consciousness, your consciousness as a preacher and the attendant consciousness of a congregation." Clarifying the term phenomenological, Buttrick states that it is his goal "to understand what may actually take place in consciousness during the production and hearing of sermons" (1987: xii). If we use the categories the authors themselves employ, Craddock's approach may be termed "inductive," Lowry's "narrative," and Buttrick's "phenomenological."

3. Orienting to the Listener. The turn toward listener-oriented preaching was formalized by the publication of Fred B. Craddock's 1971 book, *As One Without Authority.* When preaching to God's people, argues Craddock, "the preacher should recognize them as the people of God and realize that his message is theirs also. He speaks not only to them but for them and seeks to activate their meanings in relation to what he is saying" (64). For Craddock the participation of the listener is critical. Indeed, the listener completes the sermon or arrives at a conclusion that is his or her own conclusion, and not just the preachers. Thus, Craddock proposes a method in which the participation of the listener is critical "not just in the post-benediction implementation but in the completion of the thought, movement and decision-making within the sermon itself" (64). Moreover, Craddock asserts that a listener-driven approach to preaching is theologically consistent with the essential character of the gospel. "It is theologically basic to the inductive method that...the listener not be viewed as totally alien to God and devoid of Godwardness" (61). While he does not want to forget that a person is a sinner, he essentially constructs a homiletic method that is based on the *imago dei,* however distorted it may be. However, it would be wrong to conclude that Craddock's approach relies only on a biblical anthropology. In his later writings, Craddock distinguishes two kinds of listeners: the listener as audience and the listener as congregation. In the former case, the preacher's point of contact is the *imago dei*, but in the latter, the point of contact is the people's memory of their identity as God's people. So Craddock writes:

> When the pastor stands among them to preach, the parishioners who have said, 'Pray for us; we do not know how to speak as we ought,' just as eagerly say, 'Preach for us; we do not know how to speak as we ought.' And when the pastor does so, the people say in their hearts, 'Yes, that is it; that is our message; that is our faith' (1985: 44).

Initially, Craddock seems to have shaped his homiletic method on the basis of an optimistic anthropology and then later shifted to shaping it on the basis of his ecclesiology (O'Day 1993: 186).

Buttrick's method is also shaped by his ecclesiology and anthropology. He notes that when preachers preach they turn around and look at "an atypical audience" (1987: 254). He insists that in-church preachers address "a being-saved community in the world" (1987: 255) and not simply human beings in the world. Since preaching is through Jesus Christ, the task of preaching is twofold: "We interpret revelation in light of being-saved, and we grasp being-saved in view of revelation" (1987: 261). Preaching builds for the being-saved community what Buttrick calls a new faith-world. God's people come to church with a world construct in consciousness that has been shaped by the world in which they live, work, and play. "What happens in preaching is that our world is transformed.... By preaching, our lives, indeed, our world constructs are located in a larger world, a world in God's consciousness of us" (1994: 80).

Having defined God's people as being saved and being in the world, Buttrick then develops a homiletic method. Since God's people are in the world, Buttrick walks out the back door of the church, studies the turbulent new age in which the church lives, notes that there is "a new emerging human consciousness," and then constructs a homiletic strategy for the presentation of the gospel to this "quite different human consciousness" (O'Day 1993: 196). He does not study how language functions solely within the being-saved community, but rather he studies how it functions generally in the larger culture. In this way he builds a homiletic strategy that is intended to form faith consciousness in both in-church and out-church listeners for "the world is structured as a shared-in-common world in human consciousness" (O'Day 1993: 204). He is convinced that when preachers preach well, people will hear. To preach well, preachers will reject the following myths: (1) People hear what they wish to hear and "bleep" what they don't want to hear. (2) Different social groups hear differently—the young, the old, the rich, the poor, women, men, black, white, and so on. (3) Faithful biblical preaching will take cues from Scripture and bypass secular rhetoric which, at best, is a clever sophistry. Who, then, are our listeners? "Above all," says Buttrick, "they are people whom, in God's grace, we love.... We care enough to find out how our congregational neighbors think and speak. We love enough to set ourselves aside and form language as a gift for them.... In love preachers apply homiletic craft in order to wrap the gospel as a gift for their neighbors" (1987: 206). As Thomas G. Long concedes, Buttrick's analysis of how faith forms in contemporary human consciousness "compels us to think long and hard about what is happening inside the heads of listeners as we preach" (1989: 103).

For Eugene L. Lowry the sermon has its origins in "itches" and aims to "scratch." "Sermons are born," says Lowry, "when at least implicitly in the preacher's mind the problematic itch intersects a solutional scratch—between the particulars of the human predicament and the particularity of the gospel" (1980: 20). Thus, every sermon should move from need to solution, from "itch" to "scratch." Clearly, Lowry's homiletical plot is intended to grab and maintain the listener's attention. So all three theoreticians embrace an approach to preaching that gives substantial attention to the listener.

4. *Defining the Sermon*. Eugene L. Lowry is convinced that there is an intimate correlation between one's definition of a sermon and one's method of preaching. "All of us," he says, "have an image of what a sermon is.... so quite unconsciously it shapes what we do and how we do it" (1985: 13). He states his own thesis about a sermon in this way: "A sermon is an ordered form of moving time." Thus, instead of ordering ideas, a sermon, for Lowry, is ordering experience. For Lowry the advantage of such a definition is that it enables the preacher to focus on the congregation that will be listening rather than on ideas represented on a piece of paper. "Knowing their existence in time," writes Lowry, "we now perceive our work as doing something with their twenty minutes of listening time. Sunday we will need to arrest their times and supplant them with another—the sermon's" (1980: 6). And for Lowry, the sermon is "a narrative art form... a sacred story" (1980: 23).

David Buttrick is convinced that sermons involve an ordered sequence. "Sermons are a movement of language from one idea to another, each idea being shaped in a bundle of words. Thus, when we preach we speak in formed modules of language arranged in some patterned sequence. These modules of language we will call "moves" (1987: 299). For Buttrick, then, sermons are pictured as scenarios, as moves in sequence, as rhetorical units strung together in a logical fashion.

5. *Shaping the Sermonic Form*. All three homileticians make major contributions to our understanding of the importance of movement in sermonic form. Eugene Lowry provides a single form for all sermons, although within the single form there are at least four design options available: running the story, suspending the story, delaying the story, and alternating the story (1989: 38-41). Nonetheless, Lowry claims sermons should be designed around the five basic movements: upsetting the equilibrium, analyzing the discrepancy, disclosing the clue to resolution, experiencing the gospel, and anticipating the consequences

(1980: 27-74). For a narrative preacher like Eugene Lowry a sermon is an ordered form of moving time. He makes numerous practical suggestions about how narrative movement can be sustained: (1) by surfacing important information as part of the story; (2) by foreshadowing what will happen by use of relevant detail; and (3) by use of interior flashback (1989: 66-70). So narrative preachers like Lowry focus not merely on the content of ideas but the movement of these ideas in homiletical time.

Buttrick's approach, unlike Lowry's, does not provide a single sermonic form but instead provides a comprehensive way to think about sermon forms as sequenced scenarios of thought, yielding a variety of structures. Buttrick explains sermon design by saying, "Sermons are a sequence of plotted moves put together in a scenario by some kind of strategy" (1987: 299). However, he does provide numerous qualifications. For example, he insists that sermon scenarios must travel in a way that is natural to human consciousness. The sequence of a sermon will be influenced not only by the biblical material but also by the ways in which human consciousness functions. Thus, preachers should favor mobile structures that "travel through congregational consciousness as a series of immediate thoughts, sequentially designed and imaged with technical skill so as to assemble in forming faith" (1981: 56).

Like Buttrick, Fred Craddock reminds preachers that to be effective they will have to make movement a "primary methodological concern...." (1971: 54). What Craddock's inductive model and Lowry's narrative model share is that one never begins with the conclusion. They both promote sermonic forms that are built around the delay of the arrival of the preacher's message. Craddock hopes the congregation will experience the shock of recognition while Lowry hopes the message will be experienced, not just reported. In both cases, the sermon is a trip not just a destination (1971: 146).

6. Focusing the Sermon. Writing in somewhat obtuse fashion, Lowry insists that preaching occurs in time understood as *chronos* and announces God's time understood as the moment when *chronos* is turned to *kairos*. Then, borrowing Niebuhr's Christ-culture language, he points to Christ transforming time and argues "the goal of every sermon is to effect that transformation—to prompt such intersection of God's time with our *chronos* and inner times that the *kairotic* event happens. When this occurs—the right time for the hearer—we understand better what Luther meant by calling faith 'an acoustical affair.'" (1985: 35-36). In a more recent work and with greater clarity, Lowry claims that he embraces an understanding of revelation as event and argues that "narrative preaching seeks not simply to report some intrinsic gospel truth, but to be the truth" (O'Day 1993: 108). For Lowry, then, the goal of the sermon is to effect human transformation in time by enabling its hearers to experience God's gracious activity in Jesus Christ. Lowry's primary focus is upon the sermon as event and hence "the goal of any sermon," says Lowry, "ought to be evocation of the experience of the Word" (O'Day 1993: 110). Thus, Lowry aims at a sermon that is an event in time, focusing on experienced gospel truth.

In *Preaching,* Fred Craddock states that the primary goal of the sermon "is not to get something said but to get something heard" (167). In *Overhearing the Gospel*, he asserts that the place to begin is with the listener experience which he calls "the alpha and omega of the whole effort" (104). Even earlier, in his book *As One Without Authority*, he argues that fundamental to his inductive method "is movement of material that respects the hearer as not only capable of but deserving the right to participate in that movement and arrive at a conclusion that is his own" (1971: 62). But in another sense, Craddock's canon for assessing a sermon is the question, does the sermon say and do what the biblical text says and does? Thus, every sermon aims to say and do what the text says and does.

For David Buttrick the sermons aim to form faith consciousness. More accurately, Buttrick states that "in sermons, we are not merely forming consciousness but, inevitably, reforming and transforming consciousness...." (1987: 298-300). Thus, Christian preaching is transformational. However, the purpose of any particular sermon, argues Buttrick, "cannot be stated in some clear single sentence as older homiletic texts suggested" (1981: 58). The crucial matter for homiletic theory in Buttrick's view is the idea of performative purpose. Biblical preaching will want to ascertain what the texts is trying to do and then the sermon will want to be faithful not only to the text's message but also to what the language of the text is doing. So what is the preacher trying to do? "Presumably preaching is attempting to form, or better to transform, the listener's world in a number of ways. Obviously preaching wants to constitute the modeled world in consciousness as God's world and to replot the several entwined stories in which we live into a larger God's story" (O'Day 1993: 201). Thus, all three homileticians embrace differing views of the goal of the sermon.

7. Mapping the Preparation Process. When interpreting the biblical text, Fred Craddock proposes a seven step procedure with the seventh step stating the message of the text in one simple affirmative sentence. For Craddock, it is important to note that the procedure of arriving at a message or, determining what to say, is distinguished from the process of designing a message or, determining how to say it. He writes: "The work of interpretation, which is the heart of arriving at a message, and the work of deciding on design and movement for framing that message into a sermon are two processes with their own integrity, their own purposes, their own skills, and their own climaxes" (1985: 124). Hence, Craddock separates the work of biblical interpretation from the work of sermon formation.

Eugene Lowry rejects the pursuit of a theme sentence in the sermon preparation process as "an unnecessary, even counterproductive, division of labor" (1989: 37). He argues that it divides the biblical work from the work of sermon formation, a process which he pictures as an hourglass on its side with the "biblical work narrowing toward the thematic sentence, which then opens into sermon formation" (1989: 36). In his opinion, it is a preparation procedure that just has not worked in his own preaching experience. Indeed, he claims that in his experience the theme sentence often did not emerge until the end of the preparation process. But more importantly, he argues that the attempt to write a thematic sentence tends to reduce the preacher's openness during the balance of the preparation process. Instead, in his latest book, *How To Preach A Parable*, Lowry proposes what he deems to be a superior approach to preparation. He sees three major preparation tasks as the basis of the sermon design: focus, turn, and aim. Once the text's "focus" has been named in a preliminary way, the "turn" in the text identified, and the sermonic "aim" sensed, then the question of sermonic form becomes the central issue (1980: 17).

In his earlier work, *The Homiletical Plot*, Lowry describes "two preliminary stages in sermon preparation prior to the stage of sermonic formation proper" (1980: 17). The first he calls "wandering thoughtfulness" and the second stage is determining "the idea to be shaped into homiletical form" (17). But how does the preacher move from generalized sermon thoughts (stage one) to a generative sermon idea (stage two)? The solution is to think relationally. Lowry writes:

> What I need for a sermon to begin 'to happen' is for me to pull my thoughts towards the intersection point between need and theme. I mean quite literally that I take my jumble of notes and divide them into two stacks on the desk—the one with problem notes, and the other with theme or answer notes. Then I try to link thoughts from one stack of ideas with the other until a relational gestalt happens (1980: 19).

For Lowry, then, a sermonic idea is born when a theme is thrown against a problem. In this way, Lowry describes the shift that occurs when the preacher moves from text to sermonic design.

Unlike Craddock who insists on a discontinuity between exegetical and homiletic method, David Buttrick unites them by attending to the performative intention of both text sermon. Buttrick writes:

> Think of approaching texts not aiming to 'take out something to preach on,' or even asking what teaching, what kernel of truth is to be found within the shell of the passage. No the question you will ask is much more likely to be, 'What's going on here?' Or, perhaps, 'What does the language want my sermon to do?' (1994: 99).

Buttrick urges the preacher to think of preaching not only as instruction but also as doing what the Scripture wants done. The sermon will need to be designed to function in the consciousness of its hearers in a way that replicates how the text functioned for its original hearers. Noting that the move from text to sermon is often left unexplained by contemporary homileticians, he explains what happens. Buttrick notes: "As we translate, study, and consider a text, the structure of the biblical passage forms a contemporary structure of meaning in our consciousness" (1987: 308-317). What we preach from, insists Buttrick, is not the Bible, at least not directly, but rather, we preach from a contemporary structure of meaning prompted by the biblical text. So, for Buttrick, the skills required to recognize the text's structure and movement will also be needed for producing a sermon that will replicate the texts intentionality.

In short, each theoretician gives ample consideration to the steps that must be taken if one wishes to implement the sermonic strategies that they propose.

8. *Connecting Theology and Homiletics*. David Buttrick is unwilling to severe homiletics and theology. Indeed, he insists that the preacher cannot even move from text to sermon without theology. He writes:

> If exegesis involves some translation of biblical imagery into theological meaning, homiletics involves a reverse procedure, namely the retranslation of theological understandings into designed, imagistic language. A preacher must be poet, exegete, and theologian simply because sermon structures must be shaped so that the language of preaching 'plays' in a theological field of concern (1994: 88).

But homiletical method *per se* is also a theological issue for Buttrick. Questions of method are not merely practical matters for him. Homiletic method concerns the issue of how to present the gospel and form faith consciousness in an age that shows a marked preference for mobile forms.

We are dealing with a major alteration in human discourse—except in preaching! The usual language of preaching is a relentlessly fixed camera, a third person, objective speech. Perhaps in the future our sermons will travel through a series of moves each with a different well-defined point of view. After all, for the sake of the gospel, preachers must attempt to speak a language designed to formfit the contemporary shape of human consciousness (1989: 103).

In Buttrick's case, the forming of faith consciousness, which is surely a theological concern, is dependent upon a particular homiletic strategy. Thomas G. Long agrees when he states that "he [Buttrick] is convinced that a sermon shaped one way forms faith quite differently from a sermon shaped another way. This makes sermon form a theological and ethical issue, and not merely a rhetorical one" (1989: 103).

Craddock also insists that homiletic method is not a theological neutral question. He is opposed to the separation of the method of preaching from a theology of preaching. He draws attention to the fact that every method of communication has an implicit theology. "Not only content of preaching," writes Craddock, "but method of preaching is fundamentally a theological consideration" (1971: 52-53). What is needed, insists Craddock, is a method that incarnates the Christian message. Of course, since he is convinced that the incarnation itself is the inductive method, Craddock proposes an inductive method in preaching. Craddock elaborates: "At the risk of sounding presumptuous, it can be said that we are learning our method of communicating from God.... That is, the way of God's Word in the world [incarnation] is the way of the sermon in the world" (1985: 52).

In similar fashion, Eugene L. Lowry attributes theological significance to the stages of his homiletical plot strategy for preaching. He insists that in the preaching event, the focus must be upon God's decisive activity and not upon what we do. He rejects sermonic forms that climax with a call to commitment, thereby placing the focus on human response. Instead, Lowry insists "the climax of any sermon must be stage four—the experiencing of the gospel" (1980: 69). In short, all three theoreticians studied give theological significance to their homiletical strategies.

Select Bibliography

Achtemeier, Elizabeth. *Creative Preaching: Finding the Words*. Nashville: Abingdon Press, 1980.

_____. *Preaching As Theology & Art*. Nashville: Abingdon Press, 1984.

_____. *So You're Looking For A New Preacher*. Grand Rapids: Eerdmans Publishing Company, 1991.

Adams, Jay E. *Preaching With Purpose: The Urgent Task of Homiletics*. Grand Rapids: Zondervan Publishing House, 1982.

Bailey, Raymond, ed. *Hermeneutics For Preaching: Approaches to Contemporary Interpretations of Scripture*. Nashville: Broadman Press, 1992.

Bartlett, Gene E. *Postscript to Preaching: After Forty Years, How Will I Preach Today?* Valley Forge: Judson Press, 1981.

Baumann, J. Daniel. *An Introduction To Contemporary Preaching*. Grand Rapids: Baker Book House, 1972.

Bellah, Robert N. *Habits of the Heart: Individualism and Commitment in American Life*. San Francisco: Harper and Row, 1985.

Best, Ernest. *From Text To Sermon: Responsible Use of The New Testament*. 2nd ed. Edinburgh: T. & T. Clark Ltd, 1988.

Blair, Burton F. "Preaching As Homiletic Plot" *Pulpit Digest* 62 (November/December 1982): 23-25

Broadus, John A. *On The Preparation and Delivery of Sermons*. 4th ed. Revised by Vernon L. Stanfield. San Francisco: Harper & Row Publishers, 1979.

Buchman, Frank. *Remaking The World*. London: Bland-ford, 1947.

Bugg, Charles B. *Preaching From The Inside Out*. Nashville: Broadman Press, 1992.

Burghardt, Walter J. *Grace On Crutches: Homilies For Fellow Travelers*. New York: Paulist Press, 1986.

Buttrick, David G. "Interpretation and Preaching," *Interpretation* 25, no. 1 (January 1981): 46-58.

_____. *Homiletic: Moves and Structures*. Philadelphia: Fortress Press, 1987.

_____. *Preaching Jesus Christ: An Exercise in Homiletic Theology*. Philadelphia: Fortress Press, 1988.

_____. *A Captive Voice: The Liberation of Preaching*. Louisville: Westminster/John Knox Press, 1994.

_____. *The Mystery and The Passion: A Homiletic Reading of the Gospel Traditions*. Minneapolis: Augsburg Fortress Press, 1992.

_____. *Preaching the New and the Old*. Louisville, Kentucky: Westminster John Knox Press, 1998.

_____. *Speaking Jesus: Homiletic Theology and The Sermon on the Mount*. Louisville, Kentucky: Westminster John Knox Press, 2002.

_____. *Speaking Parables: A Homiletic Guide*. Louisville, Kentucky: Westminster John Knox Press, 2000.

Cox,　James W. "How Useful Is Inductive Preaching." *Pulpit Digest* (May/June 1990): 62-70.

Craddock, Fred B. *As One Without Authority: Essays on*

Inductive Preaching. Enid: Phillips University Press, 1971.

_____. "Recent New Testament Interpretation and Preaching," *The Princeton Seminary Bulletin.*66, no. 1 (October 1973): 76-82.

_____. *Overhearing the Gospel: Preaching and Teaching the Gospel To Those Who Have Already Heard.* Nashville: Abingdon Press, 1978.

_____."Praying Through Clenched Teeth," *The Twentieth Century Pulpit*, ed. James W. Cox, 47-52. Nashville: Abingdon Press, 1981.

_____. "Occasion-Text-Sermon" *Interpretation* 35, no. 1. (January 1981): 59-71.

_____. *The Gospels.* Nashville: Abingdon Press, 1981.

_____. *Preaching.* Nashville: Abingdon Press, 1985.

_____. "The Sermon and the Uses of Scripture," *Theology Today* 42, no. 1 (April 1985): 7-14.

_____. *Preaching: Getting Into The Text.* Produced by Emory University, 1986. Published by Abingdon Press in cooperation with Candler School of Theology, Emory University, Atlanta, Georgia. 29 minutes, 30 seconds. Videocassette.

_____. *Preaching: Getting Out of The Text.* Produced by Emory University, 1986. Published by Abingdon Press in cooperation with Candler School of Theology, Emory University, Atlanta, Georgia. 29 minutes, 30 seconds. Videocassette.

_____. *Preaching: Arriving At a Message.* Produced by Emory University, 1986. Published by Abingdon Press in cooperation with Candler School of Theology,

Emory University, Atlanta, Georgia. 30 minutes, 22 seconds. Videocassette.

_____. *Preaching: Designing the Sermon*. Produced by Emory University, 1986. Published by Abingdon Press in cooperation with Candler School of Theology, Emory University, Atlanta, Georgia. 29 minutes, 30 seconds. Videocassette.

_____. "A Preaching Interview with Fred B. Craddock." Interview by R. Albert Mohler. *Preaching* (March/April 1988): 3-6.

_____. *Interpretation, Luke: A Bible Commentary for Teaching and Preaching*. eds., James L. Mays, Patrick D. Miller, Paul J. Achtemeier. Atlanta: John Knox Press, 1990.

Crum, Milton, Jr. *Manual on Preaching*. Valley Forge: Judson Press, 1977.

Davidson, J.A. "Things To Be Understood and Things To Be Done." *Expository Times* 94 (1982-83): 306.

Davis, Henry Grady. *Design For Preaching*. Philadelphia: Fortress Press, 1958.

Dodd, C. H. *The Apostolic Preaching and Its Developments*. London: Hodder and Stoughton, 1936.

Duduit, Michael, ed. *Handbook of Contemporary Preaching*. Nashville: Broadman Press, 1992.

Duke, Robert W. *The Sermon As God's Word: Theologies for Preaching*. Abingdon Preacher's Library, ed. William D. Thompson, no.6. Nashville: Abingdon Press, 1980.

Eslinger, Richard. *A New Hearing: Living Options in Homiletic Method*. Nashville: Abingdon Press, 1987.

Eslinger, Richard, ed. *Intersections: Post-Critical Studies in Preaching*. Grand Rapids: Eerdmans Publishing Company, 1994.

Fant, Clyde E. *Preaching For Today*. San Francisco: Harper & Row, 1987.

Fee, Gordon D. *New Testament Exegesis*. Philadelphia: The Westminster Press, 1983.

_____. "Laos and Leadership Under The New Covenant." *Crux* Volume XXV, No. 4 (December 1989): 3-13.

Fiorenza, Elizabeth Schlussler. "A Feminist Critical Interpretation for Liberation: Martha and Mary: Luke 10:38-42." *RIL* 3 (1986): 21-36.

_____. "Theological Criteria and Historical Reconstruction: Martha and Mary: Luke 10:38-42." *CHSP* 53 (1987): 1-12.

Freeman, Harold. *Variety in Biblical Preaching: Innovative Techniques and Fresh Forms*. Waco: Word Books, 1987.

Gowan, Donald E. *Reclaiming the Old Testament for the Christian Pulpit*. Atlanta: John Knox Press, 1980.

Greidanus, Sidney. *The Modern Preacher and The Ancient Text: Interpreting and Preaching Biblical Literature*. Grand Rapids: Eerdmans Publishing Company, 1988.

Hamilton, Donald L. *Homiletical Handbook*. Nashville: Broadman Press, 1992.

Hobbie, F. Wellford. "The Play Is the Thing: New Forms for the Sermon," *Journal for Preachers* 5, no. 4 (1982): 17-23.

Holbert, John C. "Narrative Preaching: Possibilities and Perils" *Preaching* (May/June 1992): 22-28.

Jenson, Richard A. *Telling the Story: Variety and Imagination in Preaching.* Minneapolis: Augsburg Publishing House, 1980.

Jeremias, J. *The Central Message of the New Testament.* Philadelphia: Fortress Press, 1965.

Karris, Robert J. *Luke: Artist and Theologian. Luke's Passion Account as Literature.* New York: Paulist Press, 1985.

Keck, Leander E. *The Bible In The Pulpit: The Renewal of Biblical Preaching.* Nashville: Abingdon Press, 1978.

Kort, Wesley. *Narrative Elements and Religious Meaning.* Philadelphia: Fortress Press, 1975.

Laymon, Charles M., ed. *The Interpreter's One-Volume Commentary on the Bible.* Nashville: Abingdon Press, 1971. S.v. "The Bible and Preaching," by David G. Buttrick.

Lewis, Ralph L. *Inductive Preaching: Helping People Listen.* Westchester: Crossway Books, 1983.

Lewis, Ralph L., and Gregg Lewis, *Learning to Preach Like Jesus.* Westchester: Crossway Books, 1989.

Lischer, Richard. "Other Voices in Homiletics" *Homiletics* 16, no. 1 (Summer 1991): 1-4.

_____. "Preaching and the Rhetoric of Promise" *Word and World* 8, no 1 (Winter 1988): 69.

_____. Review of Preaching, by Fred B. Craddock. *Interpretation* 41, no. 1 (January 1987): 190-193.

_____. *A Theology of Preaching: The Dynamics of the Gospel.* Abingdon Preacher's Library, ed. William D. Thompson, no.11. Nashville: Abingdon Press, 1981

Long, Thomas G. Review of Homiletic: Moves and Structures, by David G. Buttrick. *Homiletic* 12, no.2 (1987): 1-5.

_____. Review of A New Hearing: Living Options in Homiletic Method by Richard Eslinger. *Homiletic* 12, no. 2 (1987): 7.

_____. Review of Homiletic: Moves and Structures, by David G. Buttrick. *Theology Today* 45, no. 1 (April 1988): 109-110.

_____. *The Senses of Preaching.* Atlanta: John Knox Press, 1988.

_____. *Preaching and the Literary Forms of the Bible.* Philadelphia: Fortress Press, 1989.

_____. *The Witness of Preaching.* Louisville: Westminster/John Knox Press, 1989.

Lowry, Eugene L. *The Homiletical Plot: The Sermon As Narrative Art Form.* Atlanta: John Knox Press, 1980.

_____. *Doing Time in the Pulpit: The Relationship Between Narrative and Preaching.* Nashville: Abingdon Press, 1985.

_____. "The Narrative Quality of Experience as a Bridge to Preaching" *Preaching* (September/October 1986): 18-24.

_____. *How To Preach a Parable: Designs for Narrative Sermons.* Abingdon Press, 1989.

_____. *The Sermon: Dancing the Edge of Mystery.*

Nashville: Abingdon Press, 1997.

McCullough, Don W. "Pulpit Moves" *Christianity Today* (January 14, 1991): 8.

MacLeod, Donald. Review of Homiletic: Moves and Structures, by David Buttrick. *Interpretation* 43, no.1 (January 1987): 82-87.

McClure, John S. *The Four Codes of Preaching: Rhetorical Strategies*. Minneapolis: Fortress Press, 1991.

_____. "Narrative and Preaching: Sorting It All Out." *Journal for Preachers* 15 (Advent 1991): 24-25.

McDill, Wayne. *The 12 Essential Skills for Great Preaching*. Nashville: Broadman & Holman Publishers, 1994.

Meyers, Robin R. *With Ears To Hear: Preaching As Self-Persuasion*. Cleveland: The Pilgrim Press, 1993.

Miller, Calvin. *Spirit, Word, and Story: A Philosophy of Preaching*. Dallas: Word Publishing, 1989.

_____. *The Empowered Communicator: 7 Keys to Unlocking an Audience*. Nashville: Broadman & Holman Publishers, 1994.

Mohler, R. Albert. Review of Preaching, by Fred B. Craddock. *Preaching* (November/December 1985): 43-44.

_____. Review of Homiletic: Moves and Structures, by David G. Buttrick. *Preaching* (September/October 1987):40-42.

_____. Review of Variety in Biblical Preaching: Innovative Techniques and Fresh Forms, by Harold Freeman. *Preaching* (May-June 1987): 46-47.

_____. Review of Doing Time in the Pulpit: The Relationship Between Narrative and Preaching. *Preaching* (March/April 1987): 42-43.

Muehl,William. *Why Preach? Why Listen?* Philadelphia: Fortress Press, 1986.

O'Day, Gail R., and Thomas G. Long, eds. *Listening To The Word.* Nashville: Abingdon Press, 1993.

Perry, Lloyd M., and Charles M. Sell. *Speaking To Life's Problems: A Sourcebook for Preaching & Teaching.* Chicago: Moody Press, 1983.

_____. *Biblical Preaching For Today's World.* Chicago: Moody Press, 1973; Revised, Chicago: Moody Press, 1990.

Pitt-Watson, Ian. *A Primer For Preachers.* Grand Rapids: Baker Book House, 1986.

Proctor, Samuel D. *How Shall They Hear: Effective Preaching For Vital Faith.* Valley Forge: Judson Press, 1992.

Rahner, Karl, ed. *Encyclopedia of Theology.* New York: The Seabury Press, 1975. S.v. "Pastoral Theology," by Heinz Schuster.

Robinson, Haddon W. *Biblical Preaching: The Development and Delivery of Expository Messages.* Grand Rapids: Baker Book House, 1980.

Robinson, Wayne Bradley, ed. *Journeys Toward Narrative Preaching.* New York: The Pilgrim Press, 1990.

Sakenfeld, Katharine Doob. *Faithfulness in Action: Loyalty in Biblical Perspective.* Philadelphia: Fortress Press,1985.

Sangster, W. E. *The Craft of The Sermon Construction.* Eppworth Press, 1954; reprint, Basingstoke: Pickering & Inglis, 1978.

Sleeth, Ronald E. *God's Word & Our Words: Basic Homiletics*. Atlanta: John Knox Press, 1986.

Stott, John R. W. *Between Two Worlds: The Art of Preaching in the Twentieth Century*. Grand Rapids: Eerdmans Press, 1982.

Thompson, W. D. *Preaching Biblically: Exegesis and Interpretation*. Abingdon Preacher's Library, ed. William D. Thompson, no. 11. Nashville: Abingdon Press, 1981

Troeger, Thomas H. "Imaginative Theology: The Shape of Post-Modern Homiletics" *Homiletic* 13, no. 1 (1988): 28-32.

_____. *Imagining the Sermon*. Nashville: Abingdon Press, 1990.

Van Harn, Roger E. *Pew Rights: For People Who Listen To Sermons*. Grand Rapids: Eerdmans Pubishing Company, 1992.

Van Seters, Arthur, ed. *Preaching As A Social Act: Theology & Practice*. Nashville: Abingdon Press, 1988.

Wall, R.W. "Martha and Mary (Luke 10:38-42) in the Context of a Christian Deuteronomy." *Journal for the Study of the New Testament* 35 (1989): 19-35.

Wardlaw, Don M., ed. *Preaching Biblically: Creating Sermons in the Shape of Scripture*. Philadelphia: The Westminster Press, 1983.

Wells, James M. "What If Peter Had Preached Deductively?" *Preaching* (March/April 1991): 40.

Willson, Patrick. Review of Preaching Jesus Christ, by David G. Buttrick. *Homiletic* 13, no. 1 (1988): 7-8.

_____. *The Practice of Preaching.* Nashville: Abingdon Press, 1995.

Wilson, Paul Scott. *Imaginations of the Heart: New Understandings in Preaching.* Nashville: Abingdon Press, 1988.

_____. "Review of How to Preach a Parable: Designs for Narrative Sermons, by Eugene L. Lowry. *Homiletic* 15, no 2 (Winter/1990): 20-21.

Yankelovich, Daniel. *New Rules: Searching For Self-Fulfillment In A World Turned Upside Down.* New York: Randam House, 1981; reprinted, New York: Bantam Books, 1982.